SLIM RANDLES

Home Country

*Drama, dreams and laughter
from America's heartland*

Rio Grande Books
Los Ranchos, New Mexico
www.LPDPress.com

Printed in the U.S.A.
Book design by Paul Rhetts

Library of Congress Cataloging-in-Publication Data

Randles, Slim.
Home country : drama, dreams and laughter from America's heartland /
Slim Randles.
p. cm.
ISBN 978-1-936744-03-9 (pbk. : alk. paper)
1. Randles, Slim. 2. Conduct of life. I. Title.
PS3568.A537H66 2012
814'.54--dc23
2012004316

For Destiny and Tony Marquez, fellow conspirators of fun and lifelong friends. For Steve Doornbos, cowboy, farrier, and teller of tales. And for Catherine, as always.

I originally named my nationally syndicated column *Home Country* because: 1. I liked the name, and 2. one of America's greatest journalists once collected his columns into a book of the same name back about the time I was born. So this is a tip of the hat to Ernie Pyle, as well.

Contents

Just where is Home Country?

Home Country is not just a place, but a state of mind. It is a place where few doors are locked and laughter can be heard at all hours.

Home Country is the friendly philosophy counter down at the Mule Barn truck stop, where Doc and Bert and Dud and the rest of the world dilemma think tank gather each morning over coffee to solve the world's problems and plan mischief.

Home Country is that swimming hole on Lewis Creek, where the children drop from the tire swing into the pool, making wet diamonds flash in the sun. And it is the old movie theater that has reverted to showing silent movies just to try to stay afloat in this age of DVD players.

Home Country is where young guys get moon eyed over young girls who can't see them for sour grapes, but they all manage to live through it, and it is the place where Dewey the Accident Prone tries many different ways of earning a living to see if he can find one that doesn't cause too much harm.

Home Country is where Sarah runs the Read Me Now bookstore and has one special category called "Love and Other Fiction." It's the place where stories travel faster than electricity and laughter outruns the stories. It's a place where a potluck supper is a major and much-anticipated social event and where a stolen garden hose is reported in the local newspaper.

This book is a collection of the best of the first five years of weekly columns. Now read by more than 1.8 million readers of hometown newspapers in 42 states, *Home Country* has become a welcome addition to life in rural America.

So just where is *Home Country*? It is here, in our hearts. It's a warm summer evening, a place by the fire in winter, a place of hope and love and sometimes tears, too. It's a place where we can be ourselves and kick off the shoes of care any time we want to.

It's home.

Spring

When the spring sun hits that certain spot on the back of
your neck and makes you leave your jacket hanging on the
fence, then it's spring. Then it is the time to build a cabin,
have a baby, start a career, write those poems, learn to bake
a soufflé, plant the garden, learn a new song, read a book
from the olden times.

3

It is the time to put those hibernating dreams back to work.

Sometimes it takes a stranger to point out our blessings. It was that way the other day down at the Mule Barn.

Everyone's aware that the old truck stop at the edge of town is a good place to eat and drink coffee, which is why it's a favorite with the locals. When the interstate came by, three miles away, we believed The Barn would be another victim of progress. But the truck drivers kept driving the extra six miles so they could sit in comfort and use the coffee cups hanging on the wall with their names on them, and gain another two pounds eating the Barn's famous chicken-fried steak ... about the size of a saddle blanket ... that would make a decent meal for any two sensible people.

Out on the interstate is the new truck stop, with showers and telephone plug-ins and an entire selection of Louis L'Amour tapes for drivers bored with driving late at night. But still many drivers detour to the edge of town and are greeted by the waitresses as family.

All we know is that's where we like to go, those of us who are married, and those of us who aren't any more or never have been. It's another of our homes.

So when Doc brought along an old medical school pal who lives in a city in the next state and introduced him to the guys, we weren't surprised. It's what we do when we like someone.

But after a couple of cups, and after repairing several gaps in the world's collective thinking, Doc's friend had this to say, and we just nodded.

"You know, when we came in here, our waitress said, 'Hi Hon. How you doing today?' She brought me a cup of coffee without my even asking. In forty years of marriage, I believe that's happened twice."

"I'm sick and tired," Steve said, putting his gear away in the tack room, "of having to think up these darn New Year's resolutions. I mean ... do I really need one?"

"I don't know," said Doc, sitting on a hay bale. "What do you guys think? Is Steve perfect yet?"

"A perfect what?" Dud chimed in.

"Okay, okay, go ahead and laugh," said the tall cowboy. "But you'll have to think up some, too, won't you?"

"That's true," Doc said. "I thought about it, and this year I'm going to quit smoking."

"You don't smoke, Doc."

"I know. That's why I think I'll be able to keep my resolution."

"You'll have to do better than that," Dud said. "I'm going to learn the accordion."

We looked at him. "Accordion?"

"Sure. You know. Myron Floren. Frankie Yankovic. 'Lady of Spain.' All that stuff."

"Accordion?"

"And why not? Isn't learning the accordion the pinnacle of human endeavor? Isn't playing polkas and waltzes the rural equivalent of grand opera? Don't the names Hohner and Galanti echo today with the same thrill as when we hear Steinway and Stradivarius?"

"No."

"Well, I'm gonna learn it anyway."

"Say Dud, can you hold off on that for about a month,?" Doc asked.

"Sure. I guess. Why?"

"So I can sell my house before the property values plummet."

Dud's face reddened in the laughter there in the barn.

"Hey," said Steve. "I'll bet ol' Dud'll be real good on that accordion, too. I'll bet he could make some money by not playing it in several night spots around here, too. Now I've been thinking, and it seems to me I should resolve to knock off a few pounds this year. I'll bet that's probably the number one resolution in the country, too."

"I'm sure you're right," Doc said. "Losing weight has to be the most popular resolution. Seems to me we must be pretty lucky to live in a country where our biggest personal failing is eating too much good food."

Spring mornings are a lot like Christmas. Each day we get up and go out into the yard, or walk along the creek or visit the horses in the pasture. And each day, each morning, we find something new the sun has brought us.

Pinfeather leaves of an unbelievable green now start showing on cottonwoods that have stood like stark ghostly frames all through the cold winter. Hopeful blades of grass peek through clumps of brown left over from last summer's verdant pasture. Everywhere we look there is something new and different.

A lot of this Christmas-in-spring is kept just among us, because we might be accused of being ... well ... poetic if we told people why we were really carrying that coffee cup out into the yard. So we say lame things like "I think I'll get some of that fresh air this morning." What we really mean, of course, is "I want to see if Richardson's bay mare has had that foal yet."

Some of us have worked very hard last fall and winter to prepare for this spring. By grafting. OK, we have a Granny Smith apple tree. Let's see if we can't get a branch of Rome Beauties or Jonagolds to grow on it, too. And we understand completely that where we live no olive tree can survive the winter. That isn't supposed to stop us from trying, is it?

Nature pitches us a boatload of challenges each day that we're alive. This plant needs more water than falls naturally here. That tree can't take the temperatures we get. This little tree needs soil with more organic matter in it.

And those challenges are the stuff winter dreams are made of. We do the best we can to cure the lack, the freeze, the drought, and then we wait for April. We wait impatiently until we can come out of the house some morning and check the grafts on the apple tree and see tiny green leaves coming on the grafted branch. We search the bare ground where we planted that new kind of seed that won't grow here - to see if it'll grow here.

It is a continuing feast of green, a triumph of anticipation. An April morning can make us want to sing.

Doc hadn't even finished loading his coffee with fake sugar before Steve piped up.

"I think it's disgusting and weird and unnatural and it should be outlawed!" the tall cowboy said, coming to rest at the philosophy counter of the Mule Barn truck stop.

"Aw Steve," said Doc, "the coffee isn't that bad."

"Coffee? Nay, I say unto you, Doc. It ain't the coffee ... it's them Academy Awards on the television. You see them? All them good-looking women Scotch-taping themselves into those dresses so they almost stay on? Those weird guys they're with who only shave on Tuesdays?"

"And this makes you angry?"

"Sure does, Doc. Those folks make a lot more money than I do and all they have to do is dress up and talk to those red carpet cameras."

"Well, Steve," said Dud, "we can do just as good as they can. Stand up."

Steve looked around and then stood slowly. Dud picked up a bottle of Tabasco sauce and, using it as a microphone, turned to the breakfast crowd in the Mule Barn.

"Good morning, folks, and we're so happy you could join us here on KRUD this morning to welcome our list of celebrities. Oh, look, it's Steve, the pride of farrier life and heavy anvils. Steve, wherever did you get that outfit?"

"Well," said Steve, grinning, "it's a creation of Levi Strauss, and please note the genuine brass rivets."

"Give us a twirl there, cowboy." And he did, to great applause.

"And your headwear today, Steve, that would be what ... Stetson?"

"Yessir. A genuine John B. Stetson original. Five ex beaver fur felt."

"The sweat stains?"

"Those were added later, actually, Dudley. A genuine cow pen fillip to offset the otherwise stunning look of my entire ensemble."

"So as not to overwhelm the onlookers, I suppose?"

"Precisely. We don't want ordinary people to think they'll never achieve this look, you see."

"An admirable pursuit," Dud said.

"*Noblesse oblige*, I believe," said Steve.

"Not until lunch," said Loretta, topping off the coffee mugs. "Breakfast special is bacon and a short stack."

When we first noticed the baby sparrow, here at the house, it saddened us all. He had fallen from his nest and was slowly walking around the front yard under the tree while his mother and father had an absolute fit.

We knew we were looking at a dead baby bird, as it was only a question of who does it, where it is done, and how long before it happens. Years of experience in these kinds of things have taught us the finality of a baby bird falling out of a tree. Would the end come from a cat, or from a raccoon wandering up from Lewis Creek, or a snake? One of the problems with being a baby bird is that almost everything with teeth wants to eat you, and if you can't fly, there's not much you can do about it. We learned that picking the baby up and putting him back in the nest wouldn't work, so we were forced to just watch his timid movements around the yard and whisper to him, "I'm sorry, pal."

You might think that the older we get, the tougher our shells become to these little natural tragedies, but it doesn't seem to work that way. Maybe it's because we've now had children of our own, and grandchildren, too. Maybe that's why it actually hurts more to see a helpless baby bird today than when we were 11 and riding our bikes on the river trails. Back then we were bulletproof, flexible, and immortal. But we learned things over the years. We saw people our age die. We saw younger people die. We accumulated our own little collection of personal tragedies.

Then the baby found the drain spout. Yep, that little rascal hopped into the drain spout coming off the roof and had sense enough to stay in there, coming to the edge of his "cave" only for meals from his anxious mother. A week later, I thought I recognized him sitting on a tree branch, looking smug. He wasn't in the drain spout and I didn't see any feathers around on the ground.

We live in an age of small miracles.

≈≈

"Well," said Steve, the tall cowboy, "at least it's Friday and we all have the weekend to look forward to."

Doc glanced up from his paper at the philosophy counter of the Mule Barn truck stop and world dilemma think tank.

"Fastest Friday you'll ever experience, Steve," said Doc.

"That's about right," said Dud.

Steve got that confounded look on his face. "What do you mean by that?"

"Today is Saturday."

"Well," Steve said, shaking his head, "that flat wrecks this day all to pieces."

"Hey," said Dud, "it's a pretty day. You have all day long to enjoy it."

"But don't you see?" Steve said, in real pain. "I was planning to spend all day Friday getting ready for Saturday and now I can't."

"Now that sounds kinda dumb," Dud said, "and I realize that, but Steve does have a point. I mean, we think in terms of time ..."

Doc groaned.

" ... yea, verily ... time and space and the continuum thereof, henceforth and forevermore. That's why, when our friend Steve here thought about Saturday, it was as though Saturday lay in the future, where things are to happen that we, as mere mortals, are loath to know..."

"Dud," said Steve, "you been watching Nova again?"

Dud blushed. "It was a good show. It concerned the string theory and fusion and the way all these marvelous things come together to make up our lives and Einstein and the total something-or-other. I forget all the little stuff, but it was pretty good. Had to do with the Big Bang and all that junk. Do you realize that when you look at a star at night, it might not be there? That star might have blown up and died a million years ago."

"So how can you tell if it's still there?" Steve asked.

"Have no idea," Dud said.

Steve grinned and tossed off the last of his coffee.

"Well, I'd better be getting along. I'm running late as it is."

"So what you up to today, Steve?" said Doc.

"Getting ready for Sunday."

When old Joe Gilliam began digging that hold in his front yard, out there close to the street, neighbors watched and wondered. When he got his grandson to help him carry the shade tree sapling from his pickup to the hole, people nodded.

Mystery solved. Old Joe's planting a tree.

After removing the root mass from the five-gallon pot, the grandson disappeared and Old Joe was left to care for the baby tree. He carefully spread the tiny feeder roots out and tucked them in with soil. Then he packed more dirt around the tree's base and soaked it well with the hose.

No one else saw anything odd in Joe planting that tree, either, but

Joe's been retired now going on 20 years. He's old and getting more frail each year. By the time that sapling gets large enough to give homes to squirrels and birds and shade to neighbors and a resting place for dogs, Joe will have been long gone.

Planting a tree is an affirmation of faith in the future. It is a gift to those yet unborn. It is a legacy of goodness, an old man's prayer.

Delbert McLain dropped in at the Mule Barn yesterday for a quick cup. He was wearing his usual suit and tie, despite the heat. Usually Delbert does his coffee drinking and socializing out at the country club where the business guys go. We've been there, and the chairs don't fit as well.

For the past 10 years now, Delbert has run the local Chamber of Commerce. The capital letters are on purpose, because that's how important it is to Delbert. We all have to admit he was a good choice. His job is to promote our town and the surrounding area, which he does by prowling through the town - his ample belly flying under a full spinnaker -looking for out-of-state plates on the cars during tourist season, and then convincing the visitors they should 1. live here forever, 2. hire locals to build them a huge house, and 3. start a business that will hire as many of us as they can stand.

According to Delbert, several things are certain about our area here: it is the only place in the world that will grow, our water is so good we don't need dentists except during our tourist season, the deer in the surrounding hills are easy to hunt and are the size of horses, the fish in Lewis Creek are so big children are afraid to swim there and our average life expectancy is right around 104.

"Boys," Delbert said with his constant grin, "it's looking like a good season. I can't tell all the details now, but it looks like we may be getting three factories and you know how many houses they'll have to build out on the flats to hold all the employees."

"Delbert," said Doc, "you know they shouldn't build out on the flats. That thing floods out about every six years."

Delbert saddened there for just a minute as he stirred his coffee, then the sales gleam relit the surface of his face.

"That's it!" he yelled. "We can call it 'seasonal waterfront!'"

Ran into Doc down at The Mule Barn the other day, so naturally we had to rid the world of about a gallon of coffee and solve the world's problems for an hour. It is the duty of all true Americans of our age, you know.

Doc said he'd been aching a little bit lately. Joints or something. He'd been out fixing the pasture fence where the mare had been pushing on it. The next morning it made him walk funny.

"I remember when my dad was my age," he said. "I asked him how it felt to be this old. Well, he looked at me as though I were committing a crime by having brown hair, you know? And then he said, "To be this old? Well, I guess it beats the alternative."

The truth is, the morning coffee drinkers of our area aren't really old, not inside. We hurt a bit more the next day when we do things, that's all. And having to walk funny for an hour or so is a small price to pay for our experience.

Being experienced sounds better.

"The other day," Doc said, "I was down to the feed store, and the kid there took one look at me and carried those heavy sacks out to the truck for me. It was embarrassing, and she shouldn't have done it."

It was the sun that did it. The sun returning, making little things want to be big things, making frozen things want to be liquid things, making sleeping things want to be stretching things. It was the sun.

That's what we figure, anyway.

That's why our resident bunkhouse cowboy, Steve, started buying nails and two by fours and going to work behind his pickup parked there on the ranch where he works. It was the sun, warming that part of the backs of our necks that stimulates the "go" process. We went over and helped him saw and nail boards together and before a week had gone by, he had an interesting looking stack of framed wall sections stacked up there.

We all knew about his obsession, of course. Steve has always dreamed of building a little cabin somewhere. It's not an unusual dream for a man whose way of life generally leads to living on other people's property and taking care of other people's livestock and other people's fences.

"I've been wanting a place," he told us one morning over coffee, "where I can go and nobody can kick me off. Nobody can fire me out of it or divorce me out of it, or anything else. A place that's paid for and I can just go there and stay there and starve if I have to. You know ... a hole-up place."

Oh, we knew. He's not the first guy to dream like that, and he won't be the last.

But nailing boards together on someone else's place didn't seem to fit the plan. We had always pictured Steve hewing away at a forest with an axe and notching up logs. But framing, it seems, is much faster, and, as Steve says, you can insulate the cabin better.

"So when are you going to put the cabin up?" said Doc, looking at the stack of nicely hammered frames.

"As soon as I get a piece of land," Steve says.

Some dreams just won't wait for escrow.

It was one of those evenings that makes you glad there's an April. Bob Milford parked his truck in front of the Mule Barn truck stop, then changed his mind and drove the few blocks into town and parked in front of Sarah's Read Me Now book store and got out.

The air was sweet like wine, warm and flowing over his body. The calves out on the Diamond W were healthy and frolicking all over the place and there had only been three difficult births where he'd had to pull the calves, and those were from first-calf heifers, so it was to be expected.

And he decided what he needed was to see how the rest of the world was waking up to spring, so he drove in from the ranch for the evening. Sarah was just locking up and visited with Bob for a few minutes before heading home for supper. Bob leaned against the wall and kept his eye on the square across the street. Two kids were playing with the cannon, shooting invisible invaders and making the world safe for suppertime in a small American town.

Dud Campbell and his wife, Anita, were walking across the square, not talking, but just being with each other. Their hands were touching, but there was more there. They were touching each other in a silent way, sharing love and promises silently. Across the way, Doc and Mrs. Doc stood together, looking in the window of the now-closed hardware store.

They looked tired tonight, Bob thought. Neither was that young any more.

Seeing these two couples made Bob a little sorry he wasn't married, but he'd tried that once and it hadn't worked out too well. She lived in the city now and was married to another fellow and had three kids.

Oh, he knew it had all happened for the best. He knew it. So he patted the cow dog in the back of his pickup and headed back down the road to the Mule Barn. He would order the special tonight. Maybe some pie, too.

Just the right thing for a warm April evening.

"I'm getting the bass buttons down now," said Dud, gleefully flipping his coffee mug to the upright and fillable position. "I'm telling you, in no time at all, I'll be able to play a waltz or polka on that thing."

"Dudley, me lad," said Doc, unofficial chief music critic at the philosophy counter, "as a physician, I am suggesting you have that accordion of yours tested."

"For what, Doc?"

"Asthma. I've heard you play it."

But there is something in the soul of an artist that cannot be dimmed by mere mortal criticism, some inner belief that if one simply practices long enough at one's craft, something good will emerge. Artists' souls are sometimes wrong.

"It's really a wonderful instrument, guys," Dud said. "I mean, think about it. With an accordion you have the equivalent of an entire orchestra. You have the treble, you have the bass, you have those stops ... you know, the switches you can flip so you can sound like everything from a church organ to a clarinet solo."

Dud looked around at the other members of the world dilemma think tank as they sipped coffee. It was a quiet morning in the Mule Barn truck stop. The rest of us were careful not to give anything away by our expressions. We know it drives Dud nuts. That's why we do it.

Finally, Steve drew himself up to his coffee-drinking pinnacle of thought. We saw he was going to say something. When that cowboy says something, it sometimes makes sense and sometimes just comes from having seen the world from between the ears of a horse. But ol' Steve was looking serious. When he's serious, he looks like a combination of

Wilford Brimley and a great horned owl.

"Would you say, Dud, that you're gaining ground on learning that 'Lady of Spain' piece?"

"Hey, Steve, I've got that sucker surrounded and I'm closing in for the kill."

"Well, I heard you worrying that thing the other day and it sounded more like 'Lady of Pain.'"

Delbert McLain, our local Chamber of Commerce, popped in the other day for coffee. Delbert's job, so we gather, is to invite huge industries to set up here, give all of us jobs, and turn this into the kind of place we don't like.

Fortunately, he's not very good at it. But we admire his trying so hard.

He and the guys at the funeral parlor are just about the only people who wear neckties in the valley. They buy them in the city.

"You look ... celebratory," Herb said.

"Thank you, Herbert," Delbert said. "It's this new idea I have. You know how that town in Pennsylvania has that Ground Hog Day, where they pull some big rat out of a hole to see if he sees his shadow?"

We did.

"Well, I don't know why we can't do it here."

"No ground hogs here."

"Prairie dogs."

Steve was looking pensive, which is hard on an old cowboy.

"Del, you really think a prairie dog cares if he can see his own shadow?"

"Why does a prairie dog stick his head out of a hole?" Del said. "To look for snakes. I figure we can call him Pete the Prairie Dog, and have National Prairie Dog Day, and each February, we can goose ol' Pete with a cattle prod or something to make him jump out of his hole and look for snakes."

"And if he doesn't see one?" said Doc.

"Well, then we'll have good fishing this coming summer."

We looked confused.

"See," Delbert said, "we can promote our local fishing and our local

prairie dogs at the same time."

Herb looked up. "Del, we don't get snakes out around here until May, so ol' Pete is never gonna see one."

"Ta-DA!" Delbert said, spreading his arms in triumph. "Which means ... what?"

"That there's always going to be good fishing here in the summer?" Doc said.

"Your honor, I rest my case!"

Steve raised his cup. "Here's to Pete the Prairie Dog and to chambers of commerce everywhere!"

We knew it was coming when Bert came into the Mule Barn truck stop the other day. He took his usual stool at the philosophy counter and world dilemma think tank, where he reigns as Cutting Edge Technology Advisor to the board of directors.

It was that glint in his eye that gave it away.

"Hi Bert."

"Hi Doc. Say, isn't this a beautiful day? It's 32 out there."

"Doesn't seem that cold," said Steve, our resident cowboy, who tends to look at everything from the back of a horse.

"Oh, not 32 degrees, dear friend ..."

Dear friend? We're in for it.

"... but 32 inches of mercury in the barometer. Winds are calm. Sun is shining. No chance of snow."

"You have a barometer?"

"Oh yeah. You can't always depend on the TV weather guy, you know. You see, it's not just where the barometer is that tells you what the weather's like, but it's where it is now in relation to where it was before. That's what they call the trend."

"Heard that word before," said Doc.

"It's scientific. Got a book about it the other day. Maizie picked it up at the library. You see, to the layman, the world outside looks kinda nice, doesn't it? Sunshine, no wind. Looks like a beautiful day. But to the expert ... to the meteorologist ... that's just the start. Oh yes. He'll look outside at the beautiful weather, but he realizes it's simply a precursor to the weather we'll have tomorrow. He'll know, you see, from how the mercury is responding in the glass ... we call the barometer a glass ... what kind of weather to expect tomorrow. That's what sets us apart from other people."

"Because you read a book?"

" ... And I have my weather station ... yes."

"So what kinda weather is coming tomorrow, Bert?"

"Oh ... 'bout like today."

"So the barometer told you that?"

Bert looked a little sheepish. "I didn't have time to figure it out. Heard it on the news."

Delbert McLain was seen going into Marvin Pincus's house the other evening. We wondered on it a bit, because those two were less likely to become friends than any other two people in the valley.

But Marvin, an old curmudgeon, is an amazing tier of fishing flies, and Delbert, who thinks blizzards are wonderful because the grass will be greener in the spring, is also an amateur fly tier. But Marvin is the real expert.

"There should be," said Del, expansively, "a National Fly Tying Month. Just think how many more people we could get to tie flies if it were more ... *organized*, you know?"

Marvin looked up from his bench and stared at his visitor over the magnifying glasses he was wearing to help him tie an Adams dry on a number 20.

"Del," he said, "some things are just meant to be quiet, you know? Just quiet. You just sit down and tie flies, and you don't need an organization or festival, or factory."

"Well ... okay, I see your point. You working on emerger patterns right now for the spring hatch?"

"Adams, dry."

Del looked over his shoulder as Marvin carefully wound the hackle behind the wings then in front of the wings, and then tied it off with a whip finish tool.

"Shouldn't you be tying emergers this time of year?"

"Del, emergers sink. Wets sink. Worms sink. Salmon eggs sink. Where's the glory in that? Dries alight on the surface film of a creek with a flutter, and they just sit there on top, going for a ride. They don't sink. Then the fish has to make an effort and come up and get him."

16   "Never thought of it that way."

Marvin nodded. "There's only dry fly fishing in the world, Del. Only dry fly fishing. Everything else is just killing fish."

Strange, Doc thought. All these years. All these people. It still hurts.

He sat by the kitchen window smelling the coffee perking and looking out at the sun rising faithfully in the east. Old Tom died around midnight, and Doc didn't get more than an hour's sleep since then. Just before he went, Tom reached out and gripped Doc's hand and thanked him for everything. He was smiling when he went.

Somehow that made it worse for Doc than just having death bring a pleasant new start for someone in pain and agony. It was Tom's time, of course. Long past Tom's time, in some ways, but Doc hadn't been able to patch him up this time. When someone Tom's age has his organs shut down, there just isn't anything a doctor can do but make him comfortable and say goodbye.

The percolator finished, and Doc knew he should go get a cup and start the day, but something made him leave the coffee behind and walk into the back yard. The buds were swelling on the fruit trees. The water in the dog dish didn't have a skim of ice this morning, either.

He would come out here later, too, he knew. He wasn't in the mood for coffee with the boys at the Mule Barn today. This will be a day where Doc, quietly and alone, will raise his coffee cup to Tom and look at the swelling buds on the fruit trees. And after 9:30, he'll be able to hear the little girls screaming happily on the playground at the school, three blocks away. Yes, he thinks that's the way to start this day, listening to the happiness of children and watching the swelling of the buds. And sipping coffee in the back yard. Just Doc and Old Tom.

Strange, Doc thought.

When the oldest Jones boy, Randall, came over to help with the chores, there was this profound sadness in his face. He moved hay with all the gusto a skinny kid just barely able to drive a car could muster, but I could tell something was wrong.

It was one of those orange sky, black tree silhouette evenings when we're glad to be alive and looking for new stars, but Randall Jones was on his own world somewhere, and it was easy to see things weren't too good on that planet.

"You feeling okay, Randy?"

He looked at me and seemed to see me for the first time. He shrugged and gave a sickly smile. "Girls," he said.

"How many?"

"Marcia Fleming."

I nodded.

"I thought you were going to ask her to the Spring Dance … what do they call it this year? Pinfeather Frolic or something?"

"Fledgling Fling," He sighed. "Well, I did ask her and she said yes, too. Had it all planned."

"And …?"

"Well, sir, you remember how we were talking a couple of weeks ago and you told me that girls like a guy who is confident? Knows what he's doing? You remember that, right?"

"Sure."

"Truth is," Randall said, "I haven't dated much. In fact … well, I've never kissed a girl. At all."

I nodded. "We all have to start sometime."

"Sure. Well, I didn't want to do it wrong, so I've been practicing by kissing my horse."

I let that image sink in. "Okay," I said. "So what went wrong?"

"When I told her about it … you know … so she'd know I was confident, she said she'd changed her mind. Now she's going with Arthur from down at the grocery store."

I just nodded. Sounds pretty dumb, like something I might've done.

The food's awfully good down at the Gates of Heaven Chinese Restaurant. The valley's other Delbert, Delbert Chin, has been putting on a decent feed there since he came to this country many years ago.

We like that lunch buffet. All you can eat, of course, and he makes this pink sauce that's out of this world. You can put it on everything. And you want to.

He asked me once why I used so much of it, and I told him if I had enough of that sauce, I could live on cardboard boxes and bedding straw.

But there's something else about Delbert, too. He is so proud of how clean his kitchen is, he will drag strangers in to look at it. We've all been in there. At least once a year, Delbert will say, "You been in my kitchen? You come look." And we do. If he doesn't recognize you as a local, you definitely will get the kitchen tour. He insists we run our fingers along the top of the stove's grease hood. We run paper towels behind the big stainless fridges. Under the stoves, too. Especially under the stoves. No grease, no dust, nothing. And he grins at the astonishment on our faces. But he keeps two teenage boys fairly busy cleaning – I mean scrubbing – that kitchen every day. You can tell when they're working, because you can hear Delbert shouting instructions.

Oh, we have the usual health inspectors, as everyone does. But they don't really need to go in there, and they know it. They'll never red tag the Gates of Heaven. At any rate, Delbert knows customers have their own ways of red tagging a place that's less than spotless, too.

One of the great pleasures of hanging around down at the livestock auction barn each Saturday morning is being able to take your dog along.

Why do we go to the sales barn? We love agriculture, and it's part of living here to see who buys what and rejoice in their good fortune, even if our own grass is stressed to the limit by whatever varmint we're currently feeding. Or, it could be that we figure we've already lived too long, and if the right horse or cow comes through there, and we buy it, our wives will see to it that we don't suffer in agony for untold years.

This weekly auction is a treasure house for our dogs. It's a dog's day out, a chance to scrounge under the bleachers for dropped hot dog portions and the occasional sweet bun crust. It's a chance for them to get reacquainted with dog buddies and to check out any new pickups in the parking lot whose tires have not yet been properly baptized.

My coonhound loves it. She had done her munching, scrounging and socializing and was curled up under my truck, waiting for me, as we were getting ready to leave. Dud's blue heeler was flitting around in the bed of his pickup truck, guarding against anything that might deign to trespass. And Doc had a new dog, of non-obvious parentage, on a leash, which meant he was not yet broken in to sales barn etiquette. Once he got used to it, and had been introduced to the other dogs, he'd fit right in and the leash would be history.

"What kind of dog is that, Doc?" we asked.

"Why, he's an Egyptian shepherd."

"I never heard of an Egyptian shepherd. Does he work cattle?"

"Nope."

"What's he do?"

Doc grinned, "He makes pyramids in the back yard."

The hassled, red-faced man cruising the neighborhood Saturday morning in the pickup truck is good ol' Bert, of course. It's a warm Saturday, which means only one thing in our part of the country – yard sales. That's why the charming lady riding next to him, his wife, Maizie, was wearing a big grin.

"There's one Bert," she said. "On the right. Pull over and park."

It took Maizie almost 20 minutes to work her way up the driveway. There were three boxes of paperback books to go through first, then a shelf full of various knobs.

"I'll ask them what these knobs are for," Maizie said.

"Don't do it," replied Bert. "If you have to ask, we don't need any."

What Bert forgot to say was that he didn't want to admit to the Johnsons, whose yard sale this was, that he didn't know what those knobs of theirs actually did.

After two paperback books, there was a little stack of doilies to go through.

"We don't need doilies," Bert said.

"Hush!" said Maizie. "People will think you aren't friendly."

Then she spotted the lamp.

It was only five bucks, and it was a golden brown like a big fat vase and had a nice amber shade on it.

"Oh Bert," Maizie said. "It's a lot like the one we used to have. Remember that one? It used to sit on the end table closest to the door to your den. I really miss that lamp. Let's get this one, Bert. It'll remind us of the one we used to have, OK?"

"It *is* kinda nice," Bert said.

Maizie bought it and Bert loaded it in the pickup, along with the new ironing board, game cartridge for the grandkids, plant pots for the geraniums, dishes for Maizie's dish collection, a serving spoon holder from Niagara Falls, and a five-gallon milk can to put magazines on.

When they got home and were unloading, Bert noticed Maizie's initials on the bottom of the new table lamp. Didn't the Johnson's buy this from them in their yard sale about 10 years ago?

Oh well, nothing shines like a new lamp, and Bert might be tired of yard saling, but he is still gentleman enough not to spoil it for Maizie.

I was recently invited to join Bob Milford, manager of the prestigious Diamond W Ranch, on a drive-around tour of the place. It's a huge, private ranch, with tiny ex-logging roads winding around through 13,000 acres of pine trees and rocks. A real paradise.

But I was horrified to see wooden street signs nailed to trees wherever two of these old logging trails came together.

"Oh no," I said, out loud.

"What's the matter?" Bob asked.

"I see you're planning a subdivision here."

Bob started laughing when I pointed at the signs. "Those are for the owners," he explained. "They live out of state and visit here one weekend a year. When they get out here, they take the pickup and drive around and get lost.

"Once I got a call on the cell phone from the owner, who said he was lost and couldn't find his way back to the house. So I asked him where he was and he said he was right there, sitting on a rock and close to a pine tree."

He chuckled. "That narrowed it down to about 13,000 acres. Well, I managed to find him, and after that, I put these signs up. I tell them now, if they get lost, to drive until they come to Home Road and then head downhill. It solved the problem."

The reporter from the big-city paper looked a bit uncomfortable as she sat at the philosophy counter of the Mule Barn truck stop. Doc ordered some coffee for her, and introduced her to the guys. She came here to interview Doc, who has been patching people up around here since the invention of pain, but there was something about her that told us she'd rather be covering the White House, and that she was determined to save the world by Tuesday at two o'clock.

"I brought you here," said Doc, "because I wanted you to see the heart of this valley, the salt of the earth, the people ... *my* people ... and the reason I've practiced medicine here all these years."

She looked at us and we tried to look earthy and salty for her.

"So you're saying," she said, "you want me to do the interview ... *here?*"

"Sure. Why not?"

"Yeah," said Dud. "Hey, if you want to know the real dirt on Doc, this is the place to do it."

"Well ... tell me about some of your most unusual cases, Doctor."

Steve whispered in Dud's ear, "If he mentions where that horse bit me on New Year's Eve, I'm out of here."

So Doc rattled off several interesting cases, without using names, and without using us, and the interview got going pretty well.

"And you deliver babies, too?" she asked.

Three of us raised our hands.

"You delivered *them?*"

"Yes ... well, I was just a kid when I did that."

We all laughed.

"Actually, I've delivered more than 4,000 babies here over the years," Doc said.

"That's amazing," said the reporter. "I didn't know there were that many people living here."

"There aren't," said Doc. "I sat down and did the numbers once, and I figure I've delivered everyone in this valley at least once."

The newspapers began disappearing about two weeks ago. Disappearing like smoke in a high wind. The paper boy swore he delivered all of them, same as usual. Same as his older brother had before him. Said he was able to "porch" quite a few, too.

But the papers kept disappearing, and it wasn't long before gab sessions were taking place in the beauty parlors and barber shops and the coffee shops regarding our local crime spree.

Theft hasn't really been a problem here, you see. Usually something that starts out looking like theft turns out to be something pretty innocent that just happened to be complicated by a lack of communication.

Oh, we're not completely free of theft, of course. Like last summer, when someone took Bert's new sprinkler off his hose in broad daylight in the front yard. For several days, Bert drove around looking at the patterns our sprinklers had, trying to locate his own. It was no use. He finally reported to us down at the Mule Barn truck stop's philosophy counter and world dilemma think tank that this sticky-fingered act of legerdemain was stacking up to be the work of a grab-it-and-git drive-by bandit from out of town.

That's why, when the copies of the Valley Weekly Miracle began disappearing from our front lawns and even from the sanctity of our front porches, we knew something had to be done. Several volunteers from the Mule Barn agreed to rise early and watch to see if their papers vanished and who did it.

This Neighborhood Watch exercise worked. Blackie was caught in the act and his crime spree ended before very many papers had vanished.

Then Blackie was taken home and his owner was informed that this was one Labrador retriever who had retrieved his last paper without paying for a subscription. Piles of newspapers were found in Blackie's house and behind the swing set.

The community was given a guarantee that on delivery mornings, Blackie would remain on the chain until everyone had their paper and coffee.

Crime cannot be allowed to continue. Especially when everyone needs to read the paper to see how much the editor dared to print.

Ran into Herb Collins the other day down by the school. He volunteers there, from time to time, helping kids with their math homework, and trying to recruit future members of The Great World of Business.

He loved business, back in the days when he lived in the city and ran the pawn shop. For years now, ever since he hung up his jeweler's loupe, he's told us that there was an excitement to making the right deal.

"It has to be right for the customer and for me, or it isn't right at all," Herb always says. "You can do that and make several people happy and earn a living. There's no need to take unfair advantage of someone just to earn a living."

Our little town is a bit tame after city life, but it's Herb's wife's home town and she wanted to come back here to live after he retired. So Herb turned to helping kids understand how wonderful business can be. He's advised kids on the most effective way of delivering newspapers on their bicycles, he's suggested advertising gimmicks for kids with summer lemonade stands, and he's helped several boys market their skills with a lawn mower. You can take the man out of the business, I guess, but it's hard to take the business out of the man.

So after the shaking hands and the how-are-yous, we talked about kids and business, and the new crop of youngsters coming up this year. I couldn't help thinking ol' Herb might jump at the chance to dive back in the world of commerce again, but he disabused me of that right away.

"All through with that," he said, shaking his head. "I was a successful businessman and now I'm successfully retired."

Successfully retired?

"That's right," he grinned. "I have a wife and a television set, and they both work."

"Good morning, Dud," Doc said.

"Nothing good about it. Nothing at all. In fact, it's a bummer all day."

"Uh oh ..."

Dud flipped his coffee cup over. "And I don't want to talk about it."

"Okay with me," Doc said.

"Me too," said Bert.

"I can wait," said Steve.

Dud waited until his cup filled with coffee. "Well, if you must know ..."

"Don't really have to," said Doc.

"Hey, I'm good, too," said Bert.

"My book got rejected," Dud said.

"Library book?"

"No ... *my* book," Dud said. "I wrote one."

"No kidding? What kind of book?"

"Murder mystery. I worked it all out very carefully before I wrote it, you know. Then I wrote it a little each day. It gave me something to look forward to. Well, I finally finished it and sent it off to this publisher. In New York, even. They sent it back. Got it back this morning."

"Sorry to hear that," Doc said. "But hey, you just send that puppy

right back out again now."

"That's right," said Steve, the cowboy of the bunch. "You get bucked off, you get right back on again."

"Been thinking, some," Dud said. "About what they wrote me. Maybe I need to work on it some more … you know, before it's ready for publication."

"They wrote you a letter and told you what was wrong with it? Hey, that's pretty nice of them."

"Well, yes, I guess so. But if I redo it the way they want it, it'll take me a long time. Months maybe."

"What was their problem with it?" Doc asked, kindly. Doc has always been a silent patron of the arts.

"They said eight murders were too many."

"Well, I for one don't think eight murders is too many for a murder mystery," Doc said. "I know other mystery writers who have had eight murders in one book and they got published just fine."

"That's true, Doc," Dud said, "but these folks said eight murders were too many in the first chapter."

The garden catalogs start coming when the snow is too deep to even find dirt. But we don't care.

This is a catalog time of year, a time for making plans and figuring out how to do something even better than we did last year.

There in the fishing catalog is that new fly-tying vise. I know I'll be able to tie flies faster and better with that, which will give me more time to cruise up and down Lewis Creek with the fly rod. Well … at least that's the plan.

And the housewares catalog has all kinds of things in it to help us peel things, boil things, slice things, and clean things. A few well-spent dollars on their 800 phone line and before you know it, our lives will be easier and our food tastier.

With the truck catalogs, we can get a little coffee maker that plugs right in to the cigarette lighter. Or we can get a little oven that plugs right in to the cigarette lighter, or a fan that plugs right in to the cigarette lighter. Let's hope the car makers continue to make cigarette lighters even after cigarettes themselves disappear. We'd miss out on a lot of fun without that plug-in.

The mule needs his catalog, too. I'll do the reading for him, and the ordering. But I think he'd appreciate one of those nice white fleece cinches. They seem so soft on an old mule's belly. And a matching saddle pad would be good, too. He's too old to rope on any more, but a guy can still appreciate comfort in semi-retirement.

The land catalogs are the most fun. In these, there are always lakes with wooded margins, begging for a little cabin. A small place where a guy can hole up and think literary thoughts and type quietly. Well, it's a thought, anyway. And that's what catalogs do, stimulate our thinking.

Spring catalogs are the novels of optimistic lives.

Delbert's at it again. You know Delbert McLain, our local chamber of commerce? He's the guy who wants to bring lots of people here so the place isn't quite as nice as it is now.

Well, ol' Delbert zipped into the Mule Barn truck stop the other day, plopped down at the empty Round Table, and motioned for those of us at the philosophy counter to join him. We did.

"Boys," he said, when we were seated and sipping, "I want to bounce an idea off you and see how it goes."

He almost whispered, "Two words … *knife sharpening!*"

"Sure," said Dud, pulling a diamond steel from a holster on his belt. "I'll sharpen it for you, Delbert."

"No, I don't mean I need a knife sharpened," he said, "I mean … a knife-sharpening contest. Actually, a knife-sharpening *fiesta. A cutlery extravaganza!*"

His face beamed, he spread his arms, his hands palms up toward Heaven as the sheer Divine magnitude of the idea settled in. Doc reached for another sugar packet.

"Just think of it, guys," Delbert said, "A veritable bevy of blade bevellers descending on our community, spending money in our restaurants, buying the latest in knife gear from the hardware store, filling the rooms at the motel."

He looked around. Steve's coffee made him cough. Doc chuckled into his hand. Dud put his diamond steel away.

"Sounds like a sharp idea to me, Del," said Doc. "I like the way you came right to the point."

"An edgy proposition," Dud said, "but one that whets the appetite."

Steve recovered from his coughing fit. "You could hold it out in the pasture and call it 'Hone on the Range.'"

Delbert ignored the groaning and smiled. "That's it, boys. Think on it. Let's come up with some good angles."

And Doc said, "I hear 10 to 15 degrees is best for a really sharp blade."

Cracker packets flew.

⌒⌒

There's something about the freedom of a motorcycle ride ... the wind blowing through your hair, passing mere cars at light speed, mosquitoes splattered against your grin. I guess that was why.

But why would ol' Dingle let Dewey Decker take his motorcycle out for a spin?

"Hey, I was right there," Dingle said later. "I told him not to go past the neighbor's mailbox, and I'd shown him how to run the thing. It's not like he wasn't supervised."

But Dewey?

The problem is, Dewey has ... *occurrences*. A Dewey Occurrence (and the capital letters are on purpose here) normally consists of something so out of the ordinary happening to him that it would be virtually impossible to happen to someone else. Like the time he got his father's pickup truck stuck in the mud. During a drought. In the only mud puddle in the county. If Dewey drove a car in the Indianapolis 500, it would be hit ... by a meteor. If Dewey took the podium to conduct the high school band on the football field at half time, the podium would disappear into quicksand. If Dewey had been a soldier in World War II, we'd all be speaking German.

So allowing Dewey to ride a motorcycle ... even as far as the neighbor's mailbox ... comes perilously close to being a crime against humanity.

You don't really think of accidents happening at less than five miles an hour. Not usually. But I understand Dingle's motorcycle can be fixed, Dewey only has to wear the cast for six weeks, and the neighbor was tired of that mailbox, anyway. The nurse down at the emergency room said she calls them "donorcycles."

⌒⌒

Doc didn't expect any patients before 10 o'clock this morning, so he was up and coffee'd and gone by 6:30. Lewis Creek. The Lunker's hole on Lewis Creek.

The Lunker is a huge rainbow trout that everyone knows about and no one has caught. So far he has resisted flies, worms, salmon eggs, spinners, and even an imitation mouse that Dud tossed in there one time just to see if the Lunker had a bass's appetite.

Fish aren't really all that bright, but the Lunker seems to deserve membership to Fish Mensa. No matter how fine the leader a guy used, it didn't fool him. Trying to figure out what to use and how to use it has fueled arguments for several years now.

But Doc thinks he has it figured out now. He has a super-fine tippet on his fly line, and used his magnifying glasses to tie a midge that is so small that if he dropped it, it would be gone forever. Doc realizes that with that fine a line, he stands a good chance of having the Lunker simply snap it off and swim away. But that would be all right with Doc if the fish just came and took that fly, because no one else had come that close to catching him yet.

And there's that wonderful new fly rod that Doc made himself from a Sage blank he bought himself at Christmas. With that rod, he believes, he should be able to feel a fish breathe in that creek.

He was in the Mule Barn before 9 a.m., holding court at the philosophy counter and told the boys what happened.

"The Lunker came up from under that big rock ledge, you know?" Doc said. "And he came within … maybe four inches of my fly as it went by."

"Four inches!" said Dud. "Hey, Doc, can you show me the pattern you tied for that?"

"Sure thing, Dud," said Doc, grinning.

Sometimes there is great glory in failure.

"I've been thinking," said Steve, the cowboy among us.

We looked at him and waited while he looked into his coffee cup. Mavis came over to give him a refill.

"I think this is the year I do it," Steve said. "I have some money saved, and I have my eye on a lot up in the hills. I believe I'll build that cabin I've been wanting."

"Sounds like fun," Doc said. We all agreed.

"If that's what you want to do, Hon," Mavis said, "you just go do it."

"Well, listen, I'd appreciate it if you wouldn't let everybody know about this yet, OK? I'm not sure I can afford it. But I'm thinking real hard on it."

"No problem, Steve," Dud said.

We all knew Steve had been nailing wall frames together in his spare time and stacking them behind the bunkhouse where he lived. Planning ahead is good.

In the next half hour, all us unofficial members of the Mule Barn truck stop's world dilemma think tank got up from the philosophy counter and did other things. I picked up a freebie paper from the rack outside, Doc walked over to see how an old man was doing who was on oxygen and sitting by himself in the corner. Dud talked to two guys from a construction crew who had come in for breakfast. They were interested in buying his pickup. All of us visited the rest room at least once, I'm sure. That's what made the mystery more interesting.

Steve was called away to the pay phone. We could hear his end of the conversation.

"Butter almond? OK. Why is that? Looks good … in the mornings. Yes, ma'am. I'll sure keep that in mind, Mrs. Miller. Thank you very much."

Steve came over and sat down. He looked at each one of us in an accusatory tone.

"That was Henrietta Miller," he finally said. "You know, the old lady who lives across from me?"

"Yes?" Doc finally said.

"She thinks I should paint the cabin's kitchen a butter almond color. She has some curtains she'll give me that will match nicely and they'll be cheerful in the mornings."

Hey, I just got a paper. My money's on Mavis.

The other night it was hot. Hot during the day, hot at night. Heat seems to define June for us, in many ways.

But in spite of that, after a day in the outdoors, we built a fire. A small fire. A "hat" fire, which mountain people define as one you can put in your hat. Why so small? Because it was hot and we didn't need the heat. Why the fire? Because we need the fire.

It is the hearth. It is the touchstone to our past. It is a link with countless generations of ancestors who have sat here looking at the flames licking up on the chunks of firewood and taking us back endless years, countless years, to what was then. Through the flames and later the glow of the coals, we can see things that we can't see at any other time. We can hear music in the crackling. We can be comforted by the fire, which is our best friend as well as a potential destroyer, at the same time.

How many times have we looked into the flames of a small fire, just like this? It's beyond counting. Sometimes the fire has been in a fireplace with all kinds of louvers and vents and controls, and yet even then we shut off the lights and sat quietly, looking into the fire and taking ourselves back to our beginnings. It is important that we do this, so important to our emotional health that we willingly pay extra for a modern city house or apartment that has a fireplace.

It doesn't make any sense at all.

No sense at all until you look into the fire and those same questions come along. Who am I? Am I doing what I'm supposed to be doing? Is my life being spent for the right things? What more can I be doing?

Do we remember other fires in faraway places? Places where the weather is different, the animals are different, the people are different. Remember using wood from other kinds of trees? Remember sitting around the fire with others who are only with us now during these quiet times by the fire and in the sanctuary of memory?

We ask ourselves these questions, but the answers can only be found in the silent glowing of the coals, and we can only hope we stack up right in the long run.

Because when we look into the coals, at the end of a long day, it's our way of going home.

When Florencio Ortiz sent off for that new slicker, everyone in town and out at the ranch knew about it. He described in detail how waterproof it was and how a cowboy just couldn't possibly get wet with this slicker on.

Then it came, and Florencio tied it behind the cantle of his saddle each day. And Florencio looked to the sky for any sign of a cloud, and then patted that slicker affectionately.

"If it rains today," he'd say, "I'm ready. Did you know this slicker keeps the saddle dry, too?"

Finally, during the gather, Florencio and the other hands were horseback about 10 miles from the truck, driving cows back to the home pasture. And the clouds came, thick and black and fast, and the rain poured.

With a joyous whoop, Florencio donned the new slicker and climbed back aboard his horse. But his buddies just sat their horses and watched. Their slickers were back in the truck.

They were amazed when Florencio dismounted, took off the slicker, tied it behind the saddle, and mounted again in the rain.

"Why?" they asked him.

"When my friends get wet," he said, "*I* get wet."

It was a lot like buzzards circling the body.

The Jones kid, Randy, was out in the Mule Barn parking lot with the hood up on his car. He was staring down into it as a first-time parachutist would look out the airplane door. You never quite knew for sure what lay ahead.

"Looks like Randy's got problems," said Steve.

"Let's have a look," said Dud.

So coffee was left to get cold and a quorum of the entire Supreme Court of All Things Mechanical – Steve, Dud, Doc, Herb and Dewey – trooped out to see what was going on.

They formed a powerful semi-circle of wisdom around the youth and his engine with folded arms and facial expressions that said, "It's okay, Kid. We're here."

Dewey spoke first. "Having trouble, Randy?"

"Won't start."

Doc, who has the most initials after his name, said, "Give it a try."

Randy ground the engine, but it wouldn't kick over.

"Stop! Stop!" Doc yelled. "Don't want to flood it."

All Doc knows about flooding is that the animals went on board, two by two.

"Randy, I think it's the solenoid," said Steve, looking wise.

"Doesn't have one, Steve," Randy said.

"Sure it does. All cars have solenoids."

"Not the new ones. Haven't made solenoids in years."

Steve's expression said, "Young punks, what do they know?" But his voice said, "Well, whattya know about that?"

"Need a jump?" Dewey asked.

"Got plenty of spark," Randy said.

Randy looked at the older men and then bent to the engine and smiled. His voice came floating up over the radiator. "Might be the junction fibrillator. Or it could be a malfunction of the Johnson switch. If I rerun the wire from the organ housing to the pump by-pass, that might get it done."

When Randy looked up, all the men had gone back in for coffee. He smiled and called Triple A on his cell phone.

"Labradoodles? Some lady in the city has Labradoodles," Doc said, putting down the paper.

"Hope it isn't catching," said Dud.

We knew without being told what a Labradoodle was, of course. It meant that a good retriever got too close to one of those tippy-toe prancing fluffs and now there are puppies that need good homes. We'd been broken in to this world by cockapoos and pekapoos, so a genuine Labradoodle wasn't that much of a stretch. At least it gave us something to talk about over coffee.

"You know," said Doc, "if you were to cross Lassie with a Cardigan Welsh corgi, you could get a colling card."

"You send that same corgi on a blind date with a shar-pei," said Dud, "and you could end up with a bunch of card sharps."

"This is getting bad ... but now that you mention it, what if a half Yorki-half old English sheepdog got interested in a lonely papillon. You'd find yourself with yoroldpappis."

The waitress was giving us looks like she needed our seats at the counter to be empty. Especially since the dog-combo disease was spreading.

"You take one of them Japanese Akitas," said a guy from the truckers' table, "and cross him with a Boston terrier, you'd get Akitaboston."

"But what would it unlock?"

"A Scottish terrier and a great Dane would produce some Great Scotts," Dud said.

"At least that would sound fairly good in a classified ad," Doc added, nodding.

"OK," said our waitress, finally succumbing to the downward spiral of waning intellect, "if you had a part saluki, part terrier and crossed it with a part bull mastiff and part Llasa apso, what would you get?"

"A litter with an identity crisis?"

"No. You'd get a bunch of ap-saluki-terri-bulls."

The groaning continued for minutes while we got refills.

"If one of them Australian dingos got crossed with those little Mexican dogs," Dud said.

We looked at him and waited.

"Well?"

We shrugged.

"You'd get a dinkahuahua, of course."

I think that's when Doc hit him with the napkin.

At least when it was over, no one had suggested a tryst between a shih-tsu and a bulldog.

There were two little boys down at the café the other day, standing outside, just waiting. They didn't have long to wait. The Greyhound bus pulls up just about one each afternoon, give or take a little.

When the bus pulled up and parked and the brakes went whoosh, those two little boys had eyes like saucers. They took in everything, from the mud on the tires to the snow clinging to the mud flaps.

The driver stepped down and helped her passengers out, proudly wearing the Greyhound uniform. She had pride in her eyes, too, as we all know how that mountain can get when it's snowing.

It's always been that way. There have always been little guys watching and wondering as the people get off for their lunch stop. Where are these people from? What was it like up on the mountain? I wonder if I could drive the bus someday when I'm grown.

When we're small, our world and our view of it tends to be smaller as well. The exotic places of the world – to an eight-year-old – aren't Singapore or Nairobi or Calcutta. The exotic places tend more toward Smithfield and Riverbank and Oakdale and Cottage Grove. At eight years old, the world's horizon is Thompson Ridge, rather than the Pacific Ocean. But that doesn't make the world any less fascinating.

Those little boys knew that, after lunch, those people would get back on that bus (they even have a restroom on the bus, you know) and they would go out of town in a diesel rush and cross the bridge on Lewis Creek and then disappear. But they know that bus will be going right past their grandparents' house in about two hours. They asked and they know. The people on that bus might be able to look out and see Grandpa's dog, Sadie, as the bus goes by.

I wonder what Sadie's doing right now? If I were on that bus right now, I could get off there and see. And someday I will. Someday I'll get on and ride and I'll know what's out there. I'll know...

There's nothing like kitchen-table guilt. From my kitchen table, I can look out on the path along the creek and see my ambitious neighbors wearing themselves out each morning. There they go, jouncing their flab along in sweatsuits and sneakers, huffing and coughing and turning red while I have a second cup of coffee.

I know. I know. I should do that. I guess I probably will, too. I've been thinking of getting one of those little radios with the ear thingies to listen to, anyway. Everyone knows that hound of mine needs her exercise, as I don't set her loose down along the river on a night coon hunt as often as I should. I might even look good in a sweatsuit.

There's a certain amount of pride a guy can take in exercise, of course. You get out in the cold morning air and suffer along in your quest to postpone The Big One as long as possible. Lots of Brownie points with the neighbors, of course, to be thought of as a with-it, "now" kinda guy. The ones who moved here from the city will begin to smile and wave more often.

The only problem with this exercise stuff is how tiring it can be. But I think I have this figured out. Yes... a plan.

I believe I'll listen to the classical station on that little radio. I think something slow by Ravel or Brahms would be just right for setting my pace. And I'll be sure to walk slowly past the neighbors' houses. You know, encourage the pity factor.

"He's been exercising so hard he's exhausted," they'll say, watching me trudge back toward the warmth of my home.

Eventually, they'll wonder why my dog hasn't lost any weight, of course, but then, no plan is perfect.

We wondered about the origin of the new sign down at the Read Me Now bookstore. Sarah McKinley has had the place for about five years now and has become a real asset to our valley. If you're looking for a book, she either has it or you don't need to read it.

She is picky, of course, and tends to buy the kind of books she thinks we should read and not always the ones we'd like to read. Fortunately for her, enough of us agree with her choices that we have kept her in business.

There's speculation about the new sign, naturally. The word got out around the valley about ten minutes after she hung it up, which is pretty slow for news to spread around here. She might have done it during a playoff game.

We all made the pilgrimage into the store to glance at it. No one was crass enough to actually ask Sarah about the wording on the sign. For one thing, it's none of our business, really. Not that that would stop us. But if we pried, that would take away all the fun we'd have out of speculating about it (sometimes known as gossip) at the barbershop, coffee shop, hair stylists and kitchens throughout the local realm.

I've heard through a good source (who swears it's true) that the sign is a direct result of a broken heart when that fellow who used to come see Sarah moved out of state. That isn't actual evidence, of course, but evidence would require asking Sarah about the sign, and that would spoil the fun.

Some say Sarah had problems with men at an even earlier age, and a few of our local ladies claim to have seen photographs in Sarah's apartment of several former swains. (Is the plural of swain *swine?*)

I've caught Sarah looking at us as we glance at the sign when we come in. I believe I've seen a semi smirk on her face at those times, too. But at any rate, I don't know of another bookstore that has a sign proclaiming one wall of books as being in the category of "Love and other Fiction."

Dud was especially quiet this morning, sitting in his usual seat at the philosophy counter of the Mule Barn truck stop. He was doodling with his napkin and a feed store ball-point pen.

Doc looked over to see if he could make it out. He couldn't. Bert adjusted his glasses.

"Murder?" said Bert.

"What?"

"You wrote murder on the napkin," Bert said. "Did I say something wrong?"

"Naw," Dud said, blushing a bit. "It's my book, that's all."

"Still having trouble trying to figure it out?" Doc said, kindly.

"The publishing company suggests I outline it first to kinda get to know where everything goes before rewriting it this time. And you know what they said about the murders…"

"Eight are too many …" said Doc.

"… in the first chapter," said Doc and Bert simultaneously.

"That's right," said Dud. "My problem is, I can't figure out who to kill first, the duchess or the truck driver."

Bert looked at Doc. "You have a duchess and a truck driver?"

"They met at the opera, or maybe the truck stop. I'm not sure yet," Dud said. "Now I need to kill both of them to make this work, you see, but then there are my other victims, and some of them really need killing pretty bad, but I'm going to have to slip those murders in a little bit at a time."

"A duchess and a truck driver?"

"Well, yeah," Dud said, "but no one is supposed to know about the affair they had back when they were both in college, see? And then when their daughter shows up …"

"The duchess and the truck driver have a daughter?"

"Sure. But she doesn't know her dad's a truck driver until after he's dead, and by then, see, she's on a killing spree… and her half brother, the dukelet, he tries to get her to join Adult Children of Murdered Parents …."

"Hold it right there!" said Doc. "I'll wait for the book. I don't want you to spoil it for me."

Saw Randall Jones the other day, walking down the street about 10 yards behind his true love, Marcia Fleming. The look in his eyes as he watched her up ahead of him was just pure pathetic. Moon-calf eyes, I think they call it.

Randy is about the most bashful high school kid when it comes to girls that we've seen since we were his age. And Marcia Fleming still wouldn't throw Randy a towel if he were drowning.

Randy, Randy. Ever since you practiced for your prom date with Marcia by kissing your horse, and then were dumb enough to tell her about it, we've been worried about you. Oh, you're a good guy and none of us older types around here would mind you asking our daughters out, if we had any. You're a good kid, sure enough. But man, are you dumb!

Marcia broke your date when you told her about the horse, of course. And you're the only guy in the valley who was surprised. You know, we'd sit down here and try to explain things to you if we thought it would help. We'd tell you that girls are human and have feelings, too, and some of them actually appreciate having a nice young fella around and interested in them. But to you, Randy, the entire world of girls, a good half the population of the world, consists of Marcia. Marcia, who haunts your dreams at night and your daydreams as you care for your animals in the afternoon. Marcia, who traps your eyes as she walks more elegantly – in your eyes – than any covey of movie starlets, beauty queens, or fashion models who ever lived. We know how it is, Randy.

But maybe one day you'll notice that nice Burchell girl, Katie, and the way she looks at you when you're busy making goo-goo eyes at Marcia. We've seen it. You see, there are a lot more Katies out there than there are Marcias, and someday you'll find one who thinks Randy Jones is the bee's knees.

After all, we found ours.

We all knew it was bound to happen, sooner or later. Dewey drives a truck like an Olympic high diver's best: headlong, full out and without looking. The accident with the grease truck was only the latest achievement of the guy who could turn a safety class into an ambulance call.

Even when he was a little kid, he could find ways of hurting himself and wrecking equipment. I swear, if someone in France threw a rock, it would hit Dewey Decker in the eye here at home.

Back in high school, Dewey once managed to get his dad's pickup truck stuck in the mud. This wouldn't be remarkable except we were in a seven-year drought and the only mud puddle in the county was the sump hole behind the laundromat. Dewey had to back up past the notions store to get there, but he found it.

He was helping us move some stock once and decided to tie up his horse and get a drink out of the creek. There were about 4,000 trees along that particular stretch of creek, but Dewey managed to tie that good sorrel mare to the only one hosting a colony of bees in its hollow trunk. They found that mare two days and ten miles later, and she wasn't in a hurry to go home.

The problem with Dewey, though, is that he's just so darn *helpful*. Being helpful - especially in this day and age - is rare enough and should be encouraged, of course. But with Dewey, you thank him for the offer of help, and then try to find him something to do that doesn't require 1. using things, 2. moving things, 3. lifting things, 4. washing things, or 5. being close to things. This tends to limit employment opportunities.

But we all understood Bob Bishop's dilemma with the grease truck. He has this old grease truck, holding more than a thousand gallons of restaurant grease. And Bob has all these pigs waiting to eat. But Bob didn't have anyone to drive the truck for him. Then Dewey, coming off a brief stint washing breakable dishes down at the Mexican restaurant, asked Bob if there was something he could do to help.

Fortunately, at that particular intersection of the interstate and the county road, no one was coming along when Dewey came by. Fortunately as well, Dewey only broke his left hand when the grease truck fell on it. Unfortunately, that intersection will be closed until someone can figure out what to do with a thousand gallons of French fry grease spread over more than an acre of pavement.

The fire department turned the hose on it, which seemed to make it more slippery. Dewey offered to use a tractor to scrape it up, which no one could picture and which offer was immediately refused.

Some of us asked Doc. He might know something we don't because of medical school. We drove out to see the spill and Doc checked it out pretty thoroughly.

"Only thing I can think of," he said, "involves two pickup loads of lettuce and a thousand gallons of vinegar."

There are some things in life that must be done alone, and Dud was feeling the brunt of that realization. It was three in the morning, and he sat at the computer, trying once again to figure things out.

The truck driver was the problem. Dud had the truck driver as the father of the girl in the novel, and the girl's mother was a duchess. That much he knew had to remain in the book. It was the classy part, you see.

He'd already cut down the number of murders in the first chapter from eight to just three, as that editor at the publishing house had suggested. Well, he hadn't actually suggested it, but was kind enough to pen "Eight murders in the first chapter seems excessive" on the bottom of the rejection slip, so Dud took it from there.

As he stared at the screen, trying to get answers from blank white spaces, Anita came up behind him and put her arms around his shoulders.

"I didn't mean to wake you, Honey," he said.

"No problem. Want some coffee?"

"I guess not."

"Couldn't you work on this on the weekend so you can get some sleep?"

Dud wanted to tell her of the burning inside, the deathless burden of the artist to produce great words that people would say generations from now. He wanted to tell her of his dream, to see his work in book stores. To sign books, to ask people how to spell their names when he inscribed something nice in each one. But that is something a guy can't even tell his wife without sounding like a pompous idiot.

"Well … tonight seemed like a good night to work on it," Dud told her.

Sometimes the things we leave unsaid almost shout at us.

It's kid time again around here. Babies everywhere. Baby trees growing in the yards, baby calves romping in the pastures, and baby humans grinning and demanding bottles and love. There are puppies toddling around the yards, kittens peeking out from under the houses where they were born, and baby birds demanding the kind of meal that would gag a sick dog off a gut truck.

Now and then one of those baby birds gets too ambitious and takes a dive out of the nest into the yard, leaving us with a problem, as we have all been told you can't touch them or the mother will reject them, but if we leave them on the ground, they'll die.

Fortunately, most babies are smart enough to stick close to home and mama and make us proud of how clever they are.

The only real problem we have with human babies is guessing which gender they are. It's a terrible thing to tell someone their baby girl is just gorgeous, only to discover it's a boy, and vice versa. The baby doesn't care, but it sure hurts mom's and dad's feelings. This whole gender identification is getting more difficult with the way our society's changing, too.

It used to be that baby boys were dressed in blue, or wrapped in a blue receiving blanket. Little girls came likewise in pink. This was a courtesy to us baby admirers, who could then tell instantly whether to call the baby handsome or pretty. But now you can't even rely on the newborn baby with pierced ears being a girl.

Now old Herb Collins is the one to show us the way on this new dilemma. Herb has been admiring babies since God made dirt, and he sailed right over this gender-identification process without missing a beat.

Whenever some young person holds up an infant these days and says, "This is my new baby, Mr. Collins," Herb takes a minute to admire the way the youngster's cheeks pooch out, and then beams and says, "Now *that's* what I call a baby!"

We all know that someone will someday find Jenkins's cabin. Oh, it's up there in those hills somewhere. We all know that.

It's become a friendly object of conjecture and speculation. No one living has seen it, as far as we know. Jenkins himself died quietly when he was on one of his infrequent trips to town for supplies. Funny guy, that Jenkins.

He worked in the city for years, mostly as a night watchman in a factory that made diapers. Didn't really enjoy people much, and told us many times how nice it was to just be in the huge factory when it was quiet. Then one day he decided to move to the mountains and make pretty things out of leather. Once in a while he'd have his coffee at the counter at the Mule Barn, but often as not, he'd camp out on the edge of town for the two or three days it took him to sell his crafts and buy
supplies. He'd smile and wave from his campsite, then he'd be gone one

morning. We wouldn't see him again for months.

Now and then someone would ask him where his cabin was, and he'd just point toward the mountains and say, "Up there." How far up there? "A ways." What was his cabin like? "Not too big."

And so we came to regard the little cabin as an intriguing mystery, an object of local legend. After he died, several of the fellows tried to backtrack him to find the place, but Jenkins evidently didn't take the same trail each time, as though he wanted his quiet times protected from even a friendly visit from one of us. During his lifetime, we respected his wishes. In this country, a man has a perfect right to be a little strange, and, truth be known, we hold a certain pride inside for those of us who seem to hear different instructions. But there is something in the human spirit that begs to have its mysteries solved, so now, several times each year, one or two of us will use the mystery of the lost cabin as an excuse to poke our noses into the nuances and seclusions of these hills.

So we play off our curiosity against our wishes to respect a man's privacy, even when he's gone. We have yet to discover Jenkins's lost cabin. Maybe we never will. Maybe that wouldn't be such a bad thing, either.

"Cuppa tea, please, Mavis," the voice said, behind us. We knew who it was, because Marvin Pincus is a rarity here in the central headquarters of coffee drinkers of the western world, better known as the Mule Barn truck stop coffee shop. He likes tea, and he doesn't come from England, either.

"Hey there, Marv," we said, and he sat.

Marvin came in on our coffee #2 this morning, so we were liquefied up pretty well and had our brains ready to come up with the perfect answers to the world's greatest dilemmas. As always.

"So, as I was saying," Doc said, "there should be some way to turn that kid's head so he could understand what makes a good and proper girl and not some fly-by-night who judges a young fella by his car."

Marvin had a sip of tea and looked at Doc. "The Jones kid?"

"Yes. What he sees in that Marcia Fleming I swear I don't know."

"Eyesight going bad, Doc?" Steve grinned. "You know darn well what he sees in her. And so does every other young man in the valley."

"Oh ... sure. She's a cutey ... but he's just wasting his life trying to get her attention. She can't see him for sour owl soup."

Randall Jones is a really decent young guy who loves his horse, his family, his community, and Marcia Fleming. But not in that order. His adoration of Marcia is second on our local list of obsessions only to Del Chin's compulsively clean kitchen down at the Gates of Heaven Chinese joint.

Del's kitchen could teach a few things to a hospital's operating room. And it smells better.

"I think maybe I can help," Marvin said.

Marvin Pincus has the reputation of being an old fly tier and reprobate, so this took us by surprise.

"Somebody call him and tell him to come by my place after chores today, will you?"

Dud shrugged. "Sure. I have his number. What are you going to tell him, Marvin?"

"That you catch more fish with substance than with flash."

Well, we had to ask, didn't we...

The Club didn't last long.

It wasn't the dues, which were nothing. It wasn't being worried about being elected recording secretary or something if you missed a meeting. There were no officers, no directors and no meetings.

It was born of an idea that occurred to Doc one day. He said the members of the Mule Barn truck stop's philosophy counter and world dilemma think tank should organize.

After his third cup, Doc turned to the others and said sitting there having coffee day after day without any real purpose just didn't seem right.

Doc said, "There are so many things a real organization can do."

"What would those things be, Doc?" Steve asked.

"Giving shoes to orphans," Doc said. "Or curing hunger in third world countries. Or we could watch TV and file complaints."

Then Dud piped up. "Would we have to wear funny hats and have a secret handshake and a password?"

"Absolutely," Doc said. "Otherwise, how would you know who was one of your brother club members and who wasn't?"

Mavis said, "What's your secret password? Regular or decaf?"

"I don't think we should let women join," said Bert.

Nobody nodded until after Mavis had topped off the cups, and had gone into the bowels of the kitchen.

"Okay," Steve said. "Let's get this straight. No meetings. No name for The Club, right? No officers. No dues to pay. All we have to do is give our shoes to some orphans, right?"

"And feed kids in third world countries."

"I don't know any kids in third world countries. Could we feed one or two around here, just to kinda e-e-e-ease into it?"

"I don't think so," said Doc. "We gotta come up with a third world country and then find out who's in charge of feeding kids. Then we can send them something."

"I move we adjourn this meeting," said Steve.

"There are no meetings," said Doc.

Since no one could name a third world country without a map or listening to National Public Radio, The Club died a quiet death then and there.

"Doc," said Mavis, topping off his cup, "I drove by your place the other day and was just marveling at your yard. Bushy and green and just … well, great."

"Thanks, Hon," Doc said, beaming.

"Only problem is," said Steve, looking up from his traditional stool at the philosophy counter, "with Doc's patented, soon-to-be-famous method of *laissez faire* gardening, it always looks the same."

"That's an outright lie!" Doc said, pretending to be a bit non-plussed. "It changes."

"Your method?" Mavis said.

Well she should ask, because our Doc told us several years ago of his new method of semi hands-off garden care. He doesn't plant anything, he doesn't water anything he isn't fond of. He just lets the yard go the way it wants to, and then uses a hoe on anything he doesn't want growing there. Usually, this means sticker bushes. He believes Nature knows what best to grow, so why fight it?

Doc has his hands full trying to keep most of us alive around here, and the rest of the time he tries to spend down on Lewis Creek giving The Lunker a hard time with his fly rod. There is little time for gardening.

Steve and Dud stared at Doc.

"What do you mean it changes, Doc?" Dud asked. He considers himself the curious one of our little group of unsung philosophers down at the Mule Barn coffee shop.

"I change out the hit list," Doc said. "For example, last year I whacked out the short puckerbrush that has those raggedy-edge leaves. This made more room for the tall, skinny stuff with the little purple flowers. Well, this year I decided I was tired of the little purple flowers, because they smell bad, so I'm whacking the tall, skinny stuff and letting those fat-leafed hoo-hoos take their place."

He looked at us. "Change is good, you know."

"I'll bet you don't know the Latin name for them," Steve said, smugly.

Doc pondered and sipped.

"Sure I do," he said. "They're *Hoohooditsia obesiana*."

"Oh Doc," said Mavis, laughing. "You just made that up."

"When they're in my yard," he said, "they play by my rules."

"He's out there again," Sharon Fleming said, looking out the kitchen window toward the alley.

"Who?" said her daughter, Marcia, while talking on the phone.

"Randy Jones."

"Did he bring the horse today?"

"Of course."

Randy Jones sat his horse in the alley and looked toward the back of Marcia Fleming's modest house near the edge of town. He had to admit that it wasn't anything special, really … the house. It was just that Marcia lived there. He looked at the unused swing set in the backyard. Naturally, Marcia wouldn't swing on it any more, or use the small slide. But it was special to Randall Jones because she had used it when she was younger.

He looked up at the back door, with the broken light fixture above it. Hey, maybe he could fix that light for them. And Marcia would come out and say "Randy, what are you doing?" and he'd say, "Just fixing your light fixture, Marcia." And then Marcia's mouth would curve into a sensuous smile and she'd say, "If you come around after dark, I'll have a special thank you for you."

Randy grabbed the saddle horn and straightened himself back up in the saddle as he felt his body start to slip.

That back door now. Marcia was now just over 17 years and four months old, Randy knew. And how many times in those years had her delicate hand reached for that doorknob ....

"Marcia, you want to invite Randy in for something cold to drink?"

"Get real, Mom. If I do that, he'll think I want to have his children and he'll come back day and night."

"You shouldn't exaggerate," Sharon Fleming said.

"You don't know Randy."

Randy's horse began to paw anxiously with a front hoof, raising sparks from the rocks in the alley. He pushed the bit out, stretching the reins from his hand. Randy ran his hand affectionately along his horse's neck and turned his head toward home.

"He's leaving," Sharon said.

"He always does," said Marcia.

Some people attend church ....

Leave it to Dewey to come up with a new idea. In some ways, it was inevitable, of course, because Dewey was so accident prone it got to the point where no one would hire him any more.

When you turn over a friend's grease truck on the interstate, and when you manage to get your dad's truck stuck in a mudhole ... during a drought ... you just plain *have* to be Dewey.

He's a good guy, and he works hard. It's just that ... well, things *happen* to Dewey. So here was a single guy in his early thirties who hadn't yet managed to whack off any arms or legs, and he was stuck for something to do. He was finally able to do some yard work trade-out at the gas station to get his dad's old pick-up running again, and Dewey was in business. But what business?

He'd talked with most of us about what kind of a job he might do that wouldn't end in disaster. No one would put him on the payroll or the company insurance plan by this time, so it would have to be something he could do on his own.

He thought at first of doing yard work, but Doc talked him out of that.

"Dewey," he told him, "before you do yard work I want you to consider several things. Lawn mowers, trimmers, hedge clippers and saws all have sharp edges."

"What you need," said cowboy Steve, seriously, "is a job where you just can't hurt anything. Especially yourself. If you have a product to sell, for example, make sure it's worth exactly nothing. That way, if you ruin it, you won't be out anything."

So Dewey gave that some thought and came up with his new idea. His pickup now says "Dewey, the Fertilizer King" on the door, along with his phone number. Each day he goes out to the dairy and to the feedlot and shovels manure into the truck, then goes to town and spreads it – for a price – in people's yards. It seems to be working so far, too.

"Only Dewey," said Doc the other day, "could become an entre-manure."

The way we heard it, it was Jim Albertson himself who did it. Jim - principal of the elementary school - Albertson. Jim Albertson, scourge of the pre-teen set. Terror of the tested.

Actually, he's a great guy, but ask an 11 year old and he'll get the shakes when his name is mentioned.

From two or three separate young reporters, this is what we were able to put together.

Before school ended for the summer, each class was paid a visit by the dreaded Mr. A.

"How many of you are honest?" he asked, looking around the room. Hands shot up everywhere.

"Then you don't mind taking a test, do you?" No one minded out loud.

He told them this would be a true-or-false quiz. They were to number their test papers from one to twenty and be ready, 'cause this was going to be fast. Then he began firing questions at them as quickly as he could, while pacing the floor ala Captain Bligh. They were to put a plus sign down for true and a minus sign for false.

Somewhere in the middle he grinned and said, "Number eleven: the moon is made of green cheese, true or false?"

There were snickers around the room, breaking some of the tension.

When the test was over, *Der Testfuhrer* told each student to correct his or her own test.

"Number one: true. Number two: true. Number three: false..."

When number eleven came up, he declared it to be true. Some of the ones who had put a minus there drew a line through it making it a plus. When everyone finished, he said, "All right now. How many of you got number eleven right? Really? That many? Well, I'll have to ask your teacher to explain that the moon actually isn't made of green cheese. That'll give you something to think about this summer, too."

Heart trouble is almost unknown among the under-twelve set. Good thing, too.

Irma has it figured out. She's a bona fide, egg-laying member of the "Production Red" hen sorority and she knows her rights.

This is really remarkable when you consider the braincase of your average barnyard chicken is wedged between some feathers and those big expressionless eyes and has about the same capacity for rational thought as that of an amoeba. But somehow this hen of mine has figured it out.

The sunlight triggers it, I believe. Sequential logic.

When the daylight comes enough to make out the outline of the house, Gunsil (the rooster) starts telling the world how wonderful he is. When the sun hits the house, The Guy Who Takes Away the Eggs comes out and puts food in the dish. When it gets dark, it's time to go back in the henhouse, better known as "Home."

She doesn't get fooled by artificiality the way Gunsil does. We've learned that a midnight visit to the bathroom is fine as long as you don't turn on the light. If the light switch goes on, out comes Gunsil from his hen-pecked existence and he begins telling the world it's time to get up and start laying.

If a person were to have several cups of coffee before bedtime, the result the next morning is a bedraggled, exhausted, confused rooster who is mad enough to want to whip the neighbor's German shepherd.

It's almost worth it.

But Irma isn't fooled by light coming through the bathroom window. She waits for the real thing. Daylight. The sun. The sun's rays slowly slide down the walls of the house until they hit the bricks of the patio. When the bricks are illuminated by the morning light, she waits exactly 17 seconds for The Guy Who Takes Away the Eggs to emerge with scratch and laying mash. Then she goes to work.

Buoyed by a sense of feminine assertiveness and egged on by an empty crop, she strides across the yard, across the patio bricks, up to the very gates of House itself, the sliding glass doors. Then Irma pecks at the glass until T.G.W.T.A.T.E. emerges with breakfast.

There aren't a lot of perks to being a chicken. One must insist on the few one has.

What happened was simple, really. Dewey did it again. Dewey is our local hard-luck case. Things just happen to Dewey. Like tying a horse to the only bee tree in six miles of forest. This little cloud hanging over him kept local businesses from giving Dewey jobs that might include machinery, money, food and sharp objects, which pretty much wipes out the local job market. Dewey decided to get his dad's old truck running, then deliver manure to people's yards from the dairy and the feedlot. This seemed to do the trick. After all, Dewey was providing a service that was worth paying him for, he was doing the dairy and the feedlot a favor by cleaning the corrals, and he was transporting goods that were worth exactly nothing.

The problem this time had to do with the latch on the main gate at the feed lot. It was worn on one side, and unless you put it all the way down, disaster loomed.

That's why Dewey blew into a full-grown panic as he was shoveling up some new raw material from the pens out there and looked up to see about 60 head of steers sauntering out onto the interstate.

It was embarrassing to Dewey, of course, but still, he should've called someone for help. Rounding up five-dozen steers over four lanes of traffic going in two directions is more than a one-man job.

Then, too, when you drive a pickup full of manure going the wrong way on the interstate, honking your horn at already panicked cattle, well …

It took six hours to get everyone back in the pens and two more days to get Dewey calmed down. No cattle were hit, no cars were damaged, and the only real loss was an estimated 600 pounds of prime beef removed by unplanned exercise.

Steve, the cowboy on the board of directors of the Mule Barn truck stop's philosophy counter and world dilemma think tank, swears on his coffee it happened.

"Tourist guy got off the train the other day when I was down there picking up a friend," Steve said. "He asked me if I was a real cowboy, and I allowed I probably was, because I wasn't smart enough to get a real job. So he asked if I minded if he asked me some questions."

Steve sipped his coffee. "I said, 'Shoot' and the guy says he wondered why we wore these big ol' hats with the wide brims. So I explained to him they give us shade in summer and keep the rain and snow off our faces, and told him we could give the horse a drink by putting water in them.

"Then he thanked me and asked why we wore chaps. So I explained how they protected our legs from cactus and thorns, you know.

"He asked about wild rags like this one," he said, touching the blue silk scarf around his neck. "I told him it filtered dust and we could tie our hats down with it in a high wind."

"Sounds reasonable," Doc said, "but I thought everybody knew that. Television and Westerns and all that."

"Well, yeah," Steve said. "Me, too. But I think this guy was from a city somewhere and didn't watch TV or eat anything that ever had a pulse. Looked kinda puny. But he was real friendly.

"So then he asked me about saddle horns. Wanted to know if they honk. This guy was really green, you know? He wanted to know about ropes and spurs, all kinds of questions like that. I did my best to answer him, too. Finally he says, 'Tell me why you cowboys always wear tennis shoes.'

"So I told him we didn't want anyone thinking we were truck drivers."

Even the truck drivers laughed at that one. Then they threw cracker packets at Steve.

Marvin Pincus heard the knock and went to answer it. He knew who it would be. This would be the Jones boy, Randall, after finishing his chores at home. Marvin had worked out how he was going to approach the issue of Randy Jones's passionate but futile worship of that glamour teen, Marcia Fleming.

"You wanted to see me, Mr. Pincus?"

"Sure did, Randy, come on in."

They went on into the den. Marvin waved Randy to a chair and put a hook in the fly tying vise.

"You know how to tie flies?"

"No sir."

"Well, son, it's a metaphor for life and love and that's why I asked you to come by today, Randy. Now watch."

The puzzled look on Randy's face remained as Marvin deftly wrapped the tail, the dubbed body and the hackle on a dry fly.

"There now, you see this fly?" Marvin took it from the vise and handed it to Randy. "This is a good pattern. A good solid pattern. This one catches fish. Regular good ol' dependable salt-of-the-earth fish. You know why?"

Randy didn't.

"Because it looks just like one of the plain ol' brown bugs that fish like to eat. Substance, you see? Substance. Now I'll tie you another one."

From the depths of the tying drawer came flashy feathers, neon hackle, bombastic tinsel and other eye-straining ingredients. Marvin soon had these festooned on a hook and looking like something between a circus clown and a lady of the evening.

"This fly," Marvin pronounced, tossing it to Randy, "is what we call an attractor. There are a number of them: Parmachene Belle, Silver Doctor, the old standby Royal Coachman and a lot more. They don't replicate any bug known to man. They catch fish, but do you know what kind of fish?"

Randy didn't.

"Foolish fish. Fish whose heads are turned by glamour and flash, rather than substance."

Marvin stood and escorted Randy to the door.

"I hope this has been educational for you, Randy. A word to the wise is sufficient, eh, guy?"

Randy still had that puzzled look on his face as he left, but he shook hands with Marvin and thanked him for the flies.

"Uh, Mr. Pincus…?

"Yes?"

"Will these work in Lewis Creek?"

It's a rare treat to have old Jasper Blankenship come down from the diggin's to stock up on supplies. And he favored us with stories at the Mule Barn this bright morning over coffee, too.

"Well, Doc," Jasper said, "you're right. I wasn't always a miner. Back during The War I had a job in the city at one of the big war plants, you know. I was a security guard and watched the gate. In those days, there was this one carpenter who just gave me the fits. He'd come out the gate at the end of the day with a wheelbarrow full of sawdust. I always stopped him and poked around in the sawdust and never found anything, but I just knew he was stealing something."

Jasper took a sip of coffee. "Well sir, four five years ago I was wetting my whistle up north a ways and this guy walked in and I knew him from somewhere so I struck up a conversation with him. Turns out he was this same carpenter guy who was wheeling that dang sawdust out the gate every afternoon. I knew this was my chance, as so many years had gone by since we both worked there.

"I told him I always knew he was stealing from the plant but could never find it in all that sawdust. I said it was a long time ago, so would he mind 'fessing up to it, just to satisfy my mind?

"He just grinned at me. So I got another round for us, and he seemed friendlier then. So I tried again. 'Come on, pardner,' I said, 'I know you were stealing something there. What was it?'"

Jasper grinned. "He smiled at me and said, 'Wheelbarrows.'"

Dud was heading home in his pickup truck when he saw the strange goings-on at the Bahdziewicz place. It's pronounced real close to bod-CHEV-itch, by the way. Abraham Lincoln Bahdziewicz was out in the family's large garden with a full compliment of kids who were happily hopping around. Some of the kids came from the neighborhood, but most of them were homegrown Bahdziewicz kids.

The Bahdziewicz family had a great garden, and went at the whole thing scientifically and in great fun, because this is one family that runs short on cash but long on kids.

Dud pulled over and watched for a minute as Abe laughingly directed the family dancers doing the vegetable boogie through the various rows of the huge garden.

"What's going on, Abe?" yelled Dud.

"Squash bug stomping time," Abe said, turning over another board

51

lying next to the vegetables. As soon as the board was flipped over, a plethora of Bahdziewicz kids stomped the bugs flat. "It's the kids' favorite time in the garden."

The third-grader, John Kennedy Bahdziewicz, said, "Flip another board, Dad."

"Hold it!" Dud yelled. "Not another move until I get back, okay? I'll be back here in five minutes. Five minutes!"

Abraham Lincoln Bahdziewicz looked at his oldest son, Woodrow Wilson Bahdziewicz, and they both shrugged. The rest of the family stopped, too. Dud peeled out in the pickup and was back in less than two minutes.

"Okay," Dud yelled. "Let's do the squash bug stomp the right way!"

And he strapped on his accordion and fired up a grand polka as boards were flipped over and the exposed squash bugs were dispatched in record polka time.

Sometimes just living here can be an awful lot of fun.

Steve, the tall cowboy of us philosophy types, was riding a young horse through town the other day to get him used to "boogers."

To gentle a horse, he explained, you give them something to booger at, and then talk them out of it. You keep coming up with new boogers and calming the horse until screaming fire engines and jet exhaust are no problem at all.

He rode up to the Campbell house and saw Anita, Dud's wife, shaking out a throw rug. The young horse began blowing nuclear snot all over the front yard and his eyes bugged out.

"Anita," Steve said, "would you mind coming over here with that rug for a minute?"

She walked slowly up to the young horse, who was crouched in the starting blocks preparing for an elliptical orbit around the sun.

"I don't want to frighten him," Anita said.

"That's why I'm here, actually," Steve said. "Would you let him smell the rug?"

She carefully and slowly held the rug up to where the colt could sniff it. He sniffed and snorted, sniffed and snorted … then sniffed, and sniffed. Then he eyed it carefully and touched it with his nose.

"If you wouldn't mind," Steve said, running his hand along the horse's neck, "could you back up about three steps and then start wiggling it?"

She backed up and gently wiggled the rug. Snort, snort, legs in starting blocks. Ready to booger.

"That's it," Steve said, calmly, rubbing the horse's neck. "Now shake it a little harder."

More snorts. More rubbing.

"Now shake it really hard."

It took the best part of a minute before the horse calmed down and just watched Anita with curiosity instead of fear.

"Thanks, Anita," Steve said. "You've helped a lot."

She looked up at him. "But why did you want me to shake a rug at him, Steve?"

"I'm thinking about getting him a job in a carpet cleaning business and want him to learn the ropes."

Summer

We get awfully hot during the day, and we shower at night now as well as in the morning. But we don't mind because the evenings are magic and make us want to live forever and sire dynasties and catch The Lunker down in Lewis Creek, just to say we did it. And in the night, while we lie in bed with the lights off, listening to music on the radio, we feel the warm breeze move the curtains and caress our skin. It is the silent blessing of summer.

No one's sure who actually saw the kangaroo first. Around this part of the country, seeing a kangaroo in an alfalfa field is not a common event.

Now the first to actually report the kangaroo to the sheriff's office was a fellow who had been spending a rather protracted, and highly liquid, evening down at the Silver Spur. He wouldn't give his name, but the dispatcher knew who he was.

Others had probably spotted the kangaroo first, but might have given some thought to just how it might sound if they reported it, and besides, he was just happily munching and hopping around out there and not bothering anyone, really, and we're not the kind of people to interfere in anyone else's life for no reason. Not even the life of a kangaroo.

The deputy couldn't locate the kangaroo, and radioed back to the dispatcher his failure. This was overheard by Jim down at the local radio station, and reported at the top of the hour. When that happened, the phone lines buzzed with people who had either already seen the kangaroo or who wanted to and wanted to know which alfalfa field he was in.

The farming area to the west of town quickly filled with families in cars, cruising around slowly, looking for the visiting foreigner. Veterinarians were called by reporters to see if anyone had a pet kangaroo who might have escaped. The zoo is 25 miles away, but it quickly counted noses and couldn't come up one kangaroo short.

The Great Kangaroo Hunt lasted until dark. Speculation lasted for days over where it had come from, where it had gone, and whether or not the coyotes would get it.

After most of a week went by with no more sightings, the kangaroo began to blend into the mists of local legend. No one had taken a photo of it, of course, but no one seriously doubted we'd had a kangaroo here, either.

Sometimes a community needs a good kangaroo sighting.

Two kids were arguing just outside my window the other day. Now that school's out, they have more time for the important issues of life, of course. This time, the subject was ghosts and whether or not they are real.

People my age have to plead guilty to the capital crime of having gray hair, and therefore aren't qualified to participate in such weighty matters.

But if they had asked me, they might have been surprised. Of course there are ghosts. We're surrounded by them.

Maybe they aren't scary or grab you from behind, but they are ghosts just the same. See that rusting tank on the edge of town? That's all that's left from when George Dodson started that tannery back in the 1920s. He was doing all right then, until the Great Depression came along, and George and the steel tank became ghosts ... a part of our history, but still somehow here with us, still a part of what makes this community our home.

Just up Lewis Creek a mile are the sloping concrete walls of what used to be a dairy. As kids, we'd sneak over ... quietly, so we didn't spook the cows ... and watch the men milking. The huge Holsteins walked in from force of habit like animated milk factories, which they were. Seems like there should be something someone could do with that old milking barn. Now it's just hard to go by and see the weeds thickening around it as it lies there in the unrelenting sun and cracks to pieces.

Down on Main Street is the old ice cream store where we used to go the very first time we had nerve enough to ask a girl to go with us. We'd bite the ends off the drinking straw covers, dip the remaining ends in chocolate syrup, and shoot them with a puff of breath to stick on the ceiling, like stalactites of young love.

But today it holds the video rental store. Times change. Businesses change. People come and then leave us. But the ghosts remain. And the ghosts are the ones who make us what we are today.

I wish those kids would ask me about them.

There is in the splashing of the creek a great spray of diamonds. As each youngster sails like an astronaut out on the tire swing, then releases the hold on the earth to flail, suspended in time and space for that brief second or two, there is a timelessness, a postponement of all things evil and destructive, an affirmation of joy.

The swimming hole in Lewis Creek has been there since Indian times, of course, and the tire swing was probably preceded by simply a rope with knots in it. It is one of the summer lodestones of our existence. Each summer we have to make our pilgrimage in the hot sun to the hole below the little waterfall, to the place were Lewis Creek widens and deepens for the benefit of hot, dry people before becoming just a creek again. And in this widening of the creek, this sacred place in our summer lives, we also play witness to the passage of years.

Across the creek from the tree with the tire swing, the gravelly bottom extends gently with almost no current for ten feet or so. This is the baby beach, where squealing tots are allowed to cool off without benefit (or hindrance) of any more covering than the smiles of their parents. As the children grow, they venture farther out into the current of the creek and test their strength against the forces of nature. By the time a youngster is eight or ten, the seduction of the tire swing becomes overwhelming and the flailing of the arms and legs against the blue of the sky begins. Later still, when gangliness becomes fluidity and sleekness, and we want to make catlike moves to attract the opposite sex, the tire is used as a swinging platform for exquisite dives into the deep part of the creek where the big trout lie in cold holes.

And as we age, and we watch our children come to love the hole in Lewis Creek, and as we sip lemonade in the shade as our grandchildren work their ways up the swimming hole chain of life, we can look at the splashing of the creek and see, with each sleek dive, with each laughing bellyflop, the diamonds of the creek sent skyward, and the laughter stays with us and keeps us strong and makes us feel rich, and fortunate.

It is unnecessary to say the hole in Lewis Creek is an important part of our lives, because it, along with so many other treasures of the years, really *is* our lives.

The Bahdziewicz clan trooped into the Mule Barn for lunch the other day, happily and noisily as only eight Americans totally in love with summer can do. The patriarch of the clan, Abraham Lincoln Bahdziewicz, led the way to a large round table and seated his wife, Sally, before pointing to which chairs the kids should use. Some people can make a celebration out of sitting down to eat, and Abe's gang knows how to do it.

The children, clockwise, were Woodrow Wilson Bahdziewicz, Betsy Ross Bahdziewicz, Neal Armstrong Bahdziewicz, John Kennedy Bahdziewicz, and Franklin Delano Bahdziewicz. Sally got a high chair for the youngest family member, Laura Bush Bahdziewicz.

We watched them order four meals for the seven of them, along with some empty plates for divvying things up. Then we took bets on whether or not they would have to ask for a "to go" box or two to take home with them. They didn't. Laura Bush Bahdziewicz had to have chocolate cream pie wiped from her face twice during dessert, too.

Before they packed up to go, Abe came over to shake hands with the members of the world dilemma think tank here at the philosophy counter. He always looks as though he's just headed home to open Christmas presents, and we envied him that wonderful zest for life.

"Abe," said Doc, when it was his turn to shake hands, "we've been wondering. You're named after a president, and all your kids are named for famous Americans."

"That's right," Abe said. "My brothers and sister, too. All of us but my wife, Sally, and I call her Sally Ride Bahdziewicz sometimes, just for fun."

"How did all that naming come about?"

"Well," Abe said, "my dad came from Poland as a kid, and the other kids at school teased him about not being a real American, you know? So he decided his kids would never have that problem. They may have some trouble pronouncing the last name, but at least they know we're Americans."

When you have a teenage relative, and the minimum age is 21 to go to a rock concert, and this relative *has* to go to the concert or die. Seriously. *Die*. Because life isn't worth living if she misses it. And, if someone under 21 can go to the concert only if an adult accompanies them. *And* ... if the only adult who will listen to the begging and the crying and the gnashing of teeth happens to be a semi-old cowboy-type Grandpa, well ... say hello to Starving Chickens.

I figured, with a name like Starving Chickens, this band probably wouldn't have the strength to do more than a few numbers before breaking for burgers and fries.

Well, that was just about as wrong a job of figuring as was the rest of my figuring. You see, I also figured the music wouldn't really hurt your ears, because they would want it to be a pleasant experience. I also figured that with three electric guitars on the stage at one time, at least one guitar player would hit the right chords. Furthermore, I figured there would be some friendly banter between the group's leader and the audience. You know, hi, how are you, having fun tonight? Now here's one of our most-requested tunes, things like that.

The older I get, the wronger I get.

Oh, the head screamer of Starving Chickens (I call him Tattoo Boy) came out to say something to all the impressionable minds waiting for his droplets of wisdom, friendship, and gratitude for coughing up admission. He looked around and then told them to do something anatomically impossible.

This brought down the house.

Impressionable Teen looked up at me with the stars of the universe in her eyes and yelled, "Oh wow! Did you hear what he *said?* And he looked right at *me* when he said it!"

Then it was two hours of throbbing before we got better. When it was over we asked each other in sign language if we had fun. One thumbs up, one thumbs down.

Sometimes you have to work to stay current with what's good in life.

It was Doc who first noticed Dud's strange behavior.

I was too busy trying to put an elk-hair caddis fly on a size 16 just beyond that big smooth rock on Lewis Creek. I know there's a big rainbow trout in that hole there, you see, and there is nothing more important, on a summer morning like this one, than enticing that big rascal into delivering himself to my waiting hands.

But Doc noticed that Dud had laid his fly rod down in the bushes and was doing strange things with his hands. Finally, Doc got my attention, pointed to Dud, and we both stopped fishing and walked over to see what our long-time pal was up to.

Dud would look around in the air, then make a one-handed grab at the air. After several grabs, he'd take two fingers of his other hand, put them in his clenched fist, and wiggle around. Then he'd smile and open his fist and look in the air again. Doc and I looked silently at each other, wondering how long it would take from our day of fishing to get Dud delivered to the nervous hospital in the city.

"Dud," said Doc, "how's the fishing?"

"Huh? Oh hi. Not fishing right now, Doc. Experimenting."

"Experimenting?" I said. Of course, I said this automatically, forgetting for a moment how time consuming it could be to start Dud explaining things of a scientific nature.

60   "Natural selection," Dud said, proudly. "Survival of the fittest. Yes, I

decided to spend my morning in Darwinian pursuits, making the world a safer place for mankind."

Doc looked at me. "He's talking like that again," he said.

"Well, Doc," said Dud, "you, of all people, should be able to appreciate what I'm doing. After all, you're a man of science and a healer. I'm going to rid the world of dangerous diseases. Observe."

Then Dud made another grab at the air, and this time we could see he was snatching a mosquito out of the air. Again he used his other hand to do something to the mosquito, and then he released it.

"I'm pulling out their drillers," Dud said. "I figgered if I pull out enough drillers, then sooner or later two drillerless mosquitoes will get married and have pups and then we'll have a family of drillerless mosquitoes here on Lewis Creek. Without drillers, they won't be able to pass along yellow fever or malaria to fishermen."

Doc looked at him in a strange way. "Dud, there's never been anyone get malaria from these Lewis Creek mosquitoes."

"See?" Dud said, brightly. "It's already working."

Life is kinda like a corrugated, washboard ranch road, I believe. Give anything enough time and experience and warts and scars and grooves will get worn in it. The down times and the up times, and the way they tend to alternate can lead to a corrugation in our dirt roads and our lives.

Any good cowboy knows how to handle a washboard road, though. Taken slowly, a pickup truck hits each little dip and rattles its carburetor until it puts a kink in the distributor clamp. It takes forever to get someplace, and the scenery never seems to change. It makes for a tedious drive to that line shack or windmill or distant pasture. Of course, it does give a guy time to compose a symphony or a letter to Congress.

Unless there is a huge hole in the washboard road ahead which needs to be avoided, there is only one way to handle a washboard road or a person's life: gun it.

Oh yeah. You step down on the pedal and kick that monster up to about 52 miles an hour and everything smoothes out. Fly, baby, fly. We hit only the high spots on the road and live a bit daringly, challenging the existence of any possible oil pan-killing rock ahead. The country slips by more excitingly and a driver tends to grin a lot.

And in life, we can wallow forever in the slow and low stuff and take ages to get somewhere, or we can floor it, give a yell, and skip along on the high spots.

Somehow, that sounds like more fun.

There's nothing quite like the advice of an old-timer to make a young fellow pay attention. No one could ever say that young Randall Jones wasn't respectful of his elders, either. That's why he was up at dawn this summer morning, down at Lewis Creek with a borrowed fly rod and ten minutes of instructions on casting. He wasn't sure exactly why Mr. Pincus told him fly fishing was a metaphor for love and life, but it does give a guy something to think about while he's fishing.

There was a reason he was given these two particular flies, and he meant to find out what it was.

He got to where he could cast out about 20 feet without getting the fly hooked in the willows, and after an hour and a change of flies, had two nice trout. That's when he looked up to see the back of a man casting long, languidly and balletically just downstream from him.

Randy watched as one watches the practiced hook of a great bowler or the curve ball of a major league pitcher. He recognized the cast. It was Doc. He walked over to watch him close up.

"Hey there, Randy," said Doc, stripping the line in on a wet fly in jerkily smooth motions. "You fishing today? Didn't know you used flies."

"Well, Mr. Pincus called me over to his place the other day …"

"Oh, that's right," Doc said, nodding. "And did he have some advice for you about girls?"

"Girls? No. He told me some trout were stupid and some trout were dependable and ugly brown bugs caught dependable fish."

Doc got a strange look on his face. "But didn't he equate this with courting girls … you know … dating, all that?"

"Dating?"

"I mean, wasn't he giving you an example of how to find a good, solid girl?"

"He never mentioned girls, Doc. He just said try the brown ugly flies for some fish and the flashy ones for others."

Doc smiled and nodded wisely. "And did that make sense to you?"

"Not until this morning," Randy Jones said, holding up his two trout.

"But now everything is clear. See these? It's obvious that foolish fish are bigger than dependable ones."

You can tell you're in a hot spell when the family canary starts to sweat, and we've sure had a canary sweater going on for a while now. If it clobbers up and promises rain, that just means it's going to be hot and humid for a while.

Miller Pond has been the most popular place in this part of the world recently, with people soaking in the water who really shouldn't be allowed in public in bathing suits. But with the heat, there has come a moratorium on good taste and we all keep cool the best we can. The swimming hole in Lewis Creek is full each day before the sun even reaches lunch time.

"I swear," said Doc the other day. It was coffee time, but he was sipping iced tea. "I swear to you here and now if I hear one more person say 'Hot enough for you?' I'll belt him!"

Dud walked in. "Hey, guys, is it hot enough for ya?"

"You want to kill him or should I?" Doc asked. "I'd do it myself, but it's too hot to move."

I was too busy sticking to my seat at the Mule Barn truck stop's philosophy counter and world dilemma think tank to get up and do anything about it, so Dud got a pass this time.

"Wonder what people did before they had air conditioning," Dud said. "Couldn't have been fun."

"Mountains," Doc said. "Or they went to the seashore. Or they worked outdoors at night."

"Ever fry an egg on the sidewalk?" Dud asked. "I tried it once, but it wasn't hot enough. I was a kid then and just got in trouble with Mom for wasting an egg."

"You know," said Doc, "I'll bet you could fry an egg on some dark metal, though. The dark color absorbs the heat and makes it hotter than the sidewalk would get. Let's get Mavis to give us an egg and we'll go try it on Dud's blue pickup."

"Let's think about it first," Dud said, laughing. "Saw a lizard carrying a canteen the other day. He wasn't sharing, either."

"You been over to the Mexican cafe lately?" Doc said. "Ol' Gilbert down there must be about as hot as the rest of us. He put a new sign up. It says, 'No Shirt, No Shoes, No Problema.'"

We laughed. "Now you know we're in a hot spell."

Everyone has his own favorite spot on Lewis Creek, I guess. Some of us favor the swimming hole below Miller's old place, with its rope swing and the kids who frolic there on hot summer days.

For Doc and Dud, it's the big race below the rocks where the huge lunker trout lives. All our efforts to catch him have so far gone unrewarded, and he keeps getting bigger each year.

But for me, there's a little cove downstream from there, shaded by huge cottonwoods and flanked in by car-sized rocks the color of wet cement. I found it sometime during a previous lifetime, I imagine. At least I can't remember the first time I discovered this place. It is walled off from the world by the rocks, protected from the sun by the cottonwoods. There is a blackened part of one overhanging rock where I've built a good many small cooking and "friendly" fires over the decades.

I've fished from there, swum from there, and ... back when the fires of spring were still racing, shared this special spot with a girl or two. But mostly it has been a private place. Everyone needs one. It's been a place to come, alone, for special times. When my dog died, when I was just a youngster, it was a place to shed private tears and remember the times the two of us had there. When the scholarship came, it was a place to come and sit by the small fire at night, a place where the noise of the water flowing by would drown out about 82 percent of my shouts of exaltation.

Years later, when my grandson's cancer went into remission, it became a very private personal church for giving thanks.

Today, it's a part of my very being ... the home place ... what Spanish-speakers would call the *querencia* ... the place of the heart. If someday my ashes could come to rest here, I wouldn't complain at all, but just smile at the sound of the creek chuckling by.

When Harley Jacobsen came into Doc's office the other day for his physical - you know, the one his wife, Gladys, insists on from time to time - it was a treat for Doc.

Harley is one of Doc's favorite people. Harley is a farmer. Not a young farmer, but a solid farmer. A 24/7 farmer. It is said in coffee-drinking circles – and we have several here – that ol' Harley can make hair grow on a bald head and wheat grow on rocks.

When he'd been thumped and bumped and listened to and pumped up and partially drained, Harley asked Doc for the verdict.

"Not bad at all for someone your age, Harley," Doc said, grinning. "But you look tired, so my advice is to take some time off and go fishing or take Gladys to the beach. Something fun. Relaxing."

"Can't right now, Doc," Harley said. "Plowing summer fallow."

"Well, how about later on?"

"There's harvest you know, and the trees will have to be pruned before winter, and then the winter wheat will go in. Have to overhaul the wheel tractor this winter and add on to the equipment shed, and then it'll be time to plant."

"Harley, I want to see you get some rest," Doc said. "You need two weeks with nothing to do. Get someone to help you and go do something fun."

"For two weeks?" Harley asked.

"Two *full* weeks, Harley."

"Doc, I just can't do the job in two weeks. Took 60 years of farming to get this tired."

Marjorie Pincus had noticed a change in her husband since the other evening. It began at supper, right after that nice Randall Jones had gone home. She didn't want to pry about what Marvin and Randy had talked about in Marvin's den, but she liked the change in her man since then.

Marvin was sitting over his second cup of tea this morning with a faraway look in his eyes and a smile. She liked that. Retirement hadn't always been easy for Marvin. He had always been a doer, and when he retired, he seemed distracted and frustrated much of the time. But now things had changed.

"Penny for your thoughts, Dear," she said.

"Just thinking," he said, smiling up at her. "That Jones boy was in need of some advice and came over the other day, you know."

She nodded.

"And I was able to straighten him out on affairs of the heart, don't you know."

"Really?"

"Oh yes," Marvin said. "He's crazy about that Marcia Fleming and she's ... well, she isn't *interested*, that's for sure. So he's just spinning his wheels. I thought it was high time someone showed him the error of his ways. There are plenty of nice girls around who would appreciate having him for a boyfriend, I'm sure. So I thought, with my experience ..."

"Marvin, I thought I was the only girl you ever went out with, all those many years ago."

"Oh, you were, Hon. You were. That's why I know the difference between a flibbertigibbet and a woman of substance. So I set him on the right path."

"I always thought you would have made a wonderful father, Marvin."

"Thank you. And you would've made a great mother, too. But now I'm thinking maybe we can share some of our experience with young people. Do you know anyone else who needs advice?"

"Not offhand, Dear."

"Well, I'm sure we'll find someone. You can't believe the difference in that young man after he compared an Adams dry to a Silver Doctor wet. I'm sure his life will be different now."

Marjorie smiled and started picking up the breakfast dishes.

"Salamander sandwiches and great Grecian toads!" said Dud, lurching into his never-really-assigned position at the Mule Barn truck stop's philosophy counter and world dilemma think tank.

Mavis stood there holding the pot of Farmer Brothers coffee as she waited for Dud to flip his coffee mug to the correct upright position.

"You want some coffee before the toads are done, Hon?" she asked.

"Sure," Dud said, laughing. "Just practicing my epithets."

Mavis poured. "When you die you want toads and salamanders on your headstone?"

"No, no, no," Dud said, in what we'd come to learn was his quasi-professorial tone. "An epithet, dear lady, is a spontaneous outburst, a grand flinging of words to the wild ether that is the very air we breathe ..."

He talks like that sometimes.

"... an expression of polysyllabic perfection designed to both stun and impress those within hearing range."

Doc looked at me. "I'm sufficiently stunned."

"Me, too."

Mavis filled everyone's cups. "Going to be one of those mornings, I guess."

"Let's get this straight," said Doc. "To stun and impress people and amaze everyone on our block, we have to talk about salamanders?"

"Of course not, Doc," said Dud. "It could be anything. Now I've just been gathering up a few of those for use later on, you see, to be used when a great epithet is called for. Let's say I walk in here one morning and you tell me the river went over its banks last night and is flooding the south valley. That would be a good time to use salamander sandwiches and great Grecian toads, you see."

"I see. The salamanders and toads because they both like water and the river overflowed, and…"

I could see the twinkle in Doc's eye.

"No," said Dud, "although you do have a good point there. But you could just as easily use an epithet like … 'Well, put Bluebeard's potatoes in a sack'!"

Doc looked at me. "Doesn't have the same stunning effect as salamander sandwiches."

I nodded.

"How about 'Dear Aunt Tillie's sainted hairnet!'"

"Better than Bluebeard's spuds, I think."

Mavis looked at us and said "Stunning."

Katie Burchell pulled over to the side of the road and put the car in neutral for a minute while she watched the young man ride down the street.

Randall Jones. Coming back from Marcia's alleyway again. Are all boys that dumb, or was Randy special? She watched him ride, proud of how he sat so straight. Katie always rode straight in the saddle, too, but there's no way Randy would ever notice.

He rode on by and smiled and waved at her, but she could see the hurt behind the smile. She returned the smile and wave and drove home.

If Randy Jones could feel that way about me … she thought … but Marcia was, well, beautiful. Katie was … pleasant? Okay? Hey, at least I'm … kind? Yep. Kind and nice.

"Randy Jones again?" Mrs. Burchell said.

"What, Mom?"

"You look so sad."

"I wish there was something I could do, that's all."

"Well, there isn't. It's up to the guy, isn't it, Dear?"

"Still, it seems like …"

Katie's dad twitched his head for her to follow him into the den. He pointed to a chair.

"Why do you like this guy, Honey?"

"He's nice to animals, he's kind to people, he … likes horses. He's devoted …"

"To the Fleming girl, right?"

"Right. No way I can compete with that."

"Ever tried? Hey, *my* daughter can do anything."

"What do you mean?"

"Does he know how you feel about him?"

"Of course not."

"Why not?"

"You mean … *tell* him? Just like *that?*"

"Why not? Some guys need a little … nudge …"

Katie hugged her dad and went to put on some makeup and change her shirt.

Outside the sky was clear, settling in toward sunset. The day looked … special. Suddenly she was in a nudging mood.

Herb Collins was back out in the yard again Saturday. The noise made the neighbors go to the windows and peek out to see what was going on, because yard work and noise and Herb have never gone together.

Mystery solved. Herb has a new gas-powered lawn mower. Last Saturday was the final outing for his quiet electric lawn mower, as he once again ran over the cord and cut it. The cord finally had more patches than a quilting bee, and Herb had opted for a gas mower that didn't require an umbilical link to the front porch.

Steve was going by in his pickup truck, the big one with duallies and the blacksmith's forge in the back, and he pulled over and stopped. Steve got out and watched quietly as Herb continued to mow the lawn. Steve poured himself a cup of coffee from his Thermos, pushed back his

Stetson, and watched Herb work up a good sweat.

Herb made three more rounds of the yard, and finally thought Steve might have something important to say to him, so he killed the engine on the mower, mopped his brow, and walked over to the visitor.

"Workin' hard there, I see," said Steve.

"Gotta stay ahead of it," said Herb.

"Why?"

Herb looked puzzled at Steve's question. "Well ... otherwise it grows too fast and the yard looks crummy."

"I was by here Thursday," said Steve. "Saw you watering."

Herb nodded.

"Why?"

"Well ... to make the grass grow, of course."

Steve raised his eyebrows.

"What?" asked Herb.

"Isn't it kinda like digging a hole and filling it up?"

"I don't get you."

Steve got back in the pickup, rolled down the window, and said. "Seems to me like you're just encouraging it."

Then he drove away, leaving Herb to once again deal with the intricacies of cowboy philosophy.

Randy Jones looked out the back window to check on his horse and saw Katie Burchell sitting there on that bay gelding of hers. The horses were talking.

"Hey, Katie," Randy said, walking out. "Want to go for a ride?"

"Not today, Randy," she said, stepping out of the saddle. "Got something else on my mind."

Randy looked perplexed. Katie blushed a little, then walked up to Randy and smiled. "I think you need a girlfriend."

"Yeah ... well, things don't always work out..."

"Not Marcia," Katie said. "Me."

Randy's mouth dropped open. "I, uh ..."

"What's wrong with me?" she asked.

"Nothing. I mean, are you sure...?"

"Sure that I like you? Sure that I want you for my boyfriend? Sure that we could enjoy going places together? Yes. Yes I am."

Randy started to smile. "You *like* me?"

"Oh yes," she said. "I have for a long time, and I'm tired of being invisible. Do you like me, too?"

"Well ... sure, I guess."

"Of course, it'll take a while for you to get used to it. Take a while for me, too. I'm not used to having a boyfriend like Randall Jones ... a guy who can do anything and is the catch of the school."

"The ...?"

"Randy, take my hand, smile at me and let's go for a walk together. We need to get used to this, okay?"

And he did. And the smile was genuine. They walked past the Mule Barn, hand in hand, looking lovingly at each other, and some of the guys ... the members of the world dilemma think tank ... were there and watched the four-legged miracle walk by.

"Well I'm dipped," said Doc.

"Isn't that the Burchell girl?" Steve said.

Doc nodded. "And about time, I'd say."

Dud looked on in amazement. "Katie Burchell. Wonder what she had to do to get his attention."

"Something, I think," Doc said, smiling, "in cast iron."

We all watched as the flag came by. It was the first thing in the parade, of course. Great big one, carried by two of the kids from the ROTC at the high school. The bands followed, along with the mounted patrol, the ski patrol in their summer-weight jackets, the float with the princesses on it, and the local kids leading dogs and cats – some rather reluctantly – on leashes.

For some of us, the Fourth of July parade is a chance to see just how much the local kids have grown over the past year. For others, it's a chance to see something that is really *ours*. This is our parade. These are our people. These are the people who make our little valley unique in the whole world. This is a chance for us all to get together and celebrate *us*, you know?

But all that comes later. What comes first on this day above all others is the American flag. Oh, it's a great big one. Where they found this one, I don't know, but it takes two high school boys to carry it. It really doesn't matter what size it is, because it's what it means to us that counts.

To Herb over there, there are memories of his terrible days in Korea, I'm sure, and the wounds that sent him home early. To Doc, maybe it's the way the G.I. Bill let him go back to college and fulfill his life's dream of taking care of sick people.

To Annette, over across the street there, there is a look in her eyes that tells us that flag meant she could protest whatever the complaint-du-jour was during her college days. She knows there are few places in the world this tolerant of unpopular opinions.

There's Dewey down on the corner. He's got his hand over his heart as the flag goes by. Maybe he's thinking of a country that will allow him to start a business with a borrowed pickup and a shovel and supply our flower beds with fertilizer. He sure hasn't been able to make anything else work for him, so far.

But these are just speculations, because what the flag means to each of us is personal. We don't have to tell anyone. We never have to explain. We even have the freedom not to be here looking as the flag goes by.

It's an American thing. A very private American moment.

Steve, the long-limbed cowboy of our band of coffee'd philosophers, rumbled into the Mule Barn coffee shop and stopped before taking his seat at the round table. He reached down, unwrapped the napkin from the fighting tools and handed his spoon to Doc.

"Here, Doc, hit me." Steve held out his hand and closed his eyes.

Doc tapped the back of Steve's hand, and Steve sat and flipped his coffee cup to the upright and fillable position.

We waited.

"You fellas know I've been looking for a little place off somewhere to build a cabin, right?"

We did.

"I bought one."

"That's great!"

"Then I called the county and they told me I had to leave a 10-foot setback on each side of the lot. Can't build on the setback, you see."

"So what's the problem?" asked Doc.

"The lot's only 25-feet wide by 100 feet deep. This means I can only build a cabin that's five feet wide."

"Well, yeah," said Dud, "but it can be ... what ... eighty feet long?

Right?"

"You can build an indoor archery range 20 yards long and still have twenty feet left over to live in," Herb suggested.

"Problem is," said Steve, "the county says the cabin has to be a minimum of 16 feet wide..."

"Meaning?"

"Well, sir," said Steve, "since I can't build on it or live on it or anything, I thought I'd just put a sign there with a collection can that says, 'Idiot's Lament. Please leave a dollar in the can.' If enough people come to look at it, I might get my money back someday..."

When the word got out about the new creation down at Delbert Chin's Gates of Heaven Chinese restaurant, the boys naturally had to go try it out.

Not that the members of the Mule Barn truck stop's world dilemma think tank are really boys ... at least not for many years now ... but they do have a boy-like curiosity about new things in our community.

Herb Collins told the coffee-drinking group about it, because his wife went to the Gates of Heaven regularly with her girlfriends.

"I'm serious, guys," Herb said.

Steve looked at him. "Delbert wouldn't do that."

"He did."

Dud looked stunned. "Sweet and sour hamburgers?"

"Yep."

"Wouldn't that make people sick?" Steve said, looking at Doc.

"Nothing Delbert would cook would *ever* make people sick," Doc replied. "His kitchen is cleaner than a hospital surgery. But sweet and sour hamburgers doesn't ... click?"

"Lunch, today?" Steve asked.

So the boys went to Gates of Heaven for lunch and they all ordered the sweet and sour hamburgers. Delbert came out of the kitchen, smiling.

"You boys don't need ketchup or mustard with these burgers," he told them. "They're fine just like they are. I have pickles, though ... you want pickles."

The burgers came, with a side order of those petrified noodles in place of French fries, and the eating began. Delbert watched their faces. He knew this was the Supreme Court of our valley when it came to introducing something new to eat.

There were nods and there were inquisitive facial expressions.

"Well?" asked Delbert.

"Del," said Doc, "your cooking is always wonderful ..."

There were concomitant nods around the table.

" ... but I think maybe I'll stick to the sweet and sour pork or shrimp. Hamburgers need ..."

"Ketchup?" said Steve.

"Mayo?" said Dud.

"Hey, they're good, though," said Doc. "I like the way the sauce gets soaked into the bun."

"That's right."

"Me, too."

"Oh shut up," said Delbert, heading for the kitchen.

"Now Steve," said Doc, "we've been giving this real estate conundrum of yours considerable thought. Sit down and flip your cup to the upright landing position and let's figure this thing out."

Steve did, and the entire population of the world dilemma think tank focused on Doc.

"You bought a lot and with the setbacks, you can only build something five feet wide, but it can be as much as 80 feet long, right?"

"Well, yeah..." Steve drawled slowly, "but to have a cabin, you have to build it at least sixteen feet wide."

"That's right, minimum of sixteen feet wide." Doc looked at the assembled as Mavis poured more coffee and brought Dewey a sweet roll large enough to use for a spare truck tire.

"Right. So Steve, here's the deal. Does it say anywhere in the rule book that it can only be one story high?"

Steve shook his head.

"That's it, then," Doc said. "You just build a cabin five feet wide and sixteen feet high. That's just two stories, right?"

"But it has to be sixteen feet *wide*, Doc."

"Wind blows up there on that ridge, doesn't it?"

Doc looked at us. "I need an amen, guys."

"Amen."

"Just tell the county the wind blew the cabin on its side."

73

Steve laughed. "But they'll look inside and see it isn't on its side."

"*Avant garde*, Steve. *Avant garde* design. You just tell them they don't have a say about interior design at all."

Doc grinned. "And *avant garde*, as we all know, is French for showing off."

Jasper Blankenship came back to his cabin from the diggin's about 11 a.m.. At his age, it doesn't make any real sense to work 12-hour days with a shovel the way he used to. For one thing, he had some money set by.

But the main reason was, Jasper just didn't look forward to the digging the way he used to, when that vein was just out of reach and maybe he'd find it the next morning. But he'd found enough, over the years. Enough.

Today his gold comes in the breaking of dawn, the mystic magic of a rainbow, and the gold-slabbed blood-red clouds of a sunset. His treasure is increased by watching the peaceful sleep of Arthur, his mixed-blood dog partner. Arthur came in from the diggin's, too, hit the kibble in his dish for two quick bites, slurped down some water, and hopped up on the cabin's single bunk, where he happily collapsed.

It was then Jasper heard the voices outside. It was a young man and woman, faces flushed with the heat of the day. They seemed surprised to find a cabin so far out in the mountains.

"Mister," said the man when he saw Jasper, "can you tell us where we are?"

Jasper chuckled. "Looks like you two could use something cold to drink. Come on in."

Their summer hike had taken a wrong turn somewhere and they had ended up at Jasper's rather than back at their car.

"We'll have a little lunch," Jasper said, "and then I'll walk you back to your car. It really isn't far, you know."

The couple relaxed then and began to enjoy Jasper's hospitality. They had to sit on the bunk, which made Arthur move down a bit, but he didn't seem to mind.

"I guess you must get social security, to live out here," said the husband.

"Well, not the kind you're thinking of," Jasper said, "because I've been working for myself since I was about 18."

"Can't you apply for it?"

Jasper thought a minute. "Let's say I was to show up at your house on a winter's night. Would you give me a meal and let me sleep on your couch?"

"Of course we would!" said the young woman.

"Well," said Jasper, "*that's* what I consider social security."

The pan-sized trout came flashing out of the water on the end of Doc's fly line, to his great surprise and pleasure, and was briefly held up in the air so a number of fellow fishermen could see how pretty he was. Then Doc gently released him.

"Pretty little thing," Dud yelled from across Lewis Creek.

"Thanks!" said Doc.

Dud and Doc are charter members of both the world dilemma think tank at the Mule Barn truck stop (and prone to coagulate morningly at the philosophy counter there) and the Lewis Creek Piscatorial Appreciation and Apprehension Society, which meets ... well ... down here at Lewis Creek.

Bert hadn't gotten a strike since he'd arrived, so he waded across and asked Doc for the secret to his success.

"Floozies," Doc said.

"What?"

"To be exact, Luther's floozies. When I go fishing with Luther's floozies, I always do well."

"Look, Doc," Bert said, "I know Luther really well, and he loves his wife. She's terrific, you know. And I'm sure Luther wouldn't..."

Doc started laughing. "No ... oh no ... here, let me show you."

And he pulled out a fly that looked like a bare fly hook with red thread wrapped around it.

"That looks like a bare fly hook with red thread wrapped around it," Bert said.

"That was my first impression, too," said Doc. "But Luther told me this is a floozy, and by golly, that's what it'll be. Here, let me give you a couple."

Bert grinned and took the flies. "Can't wait to tell Maizie I went fishing with Luther's floozies. That'll tune the old girl up something fierce!"

"Sanctimonious siphons, it's hot!" said Dud, sitting at the philosophy counter and turning over his coffee cup for action with a single smooth move.

"Epithet time again, Dudley?" said Doc.

"Epithets and heat time, Doc. When that heat comes along, the only thing that can really change an attitude is a properly tuned epithet. It's man's emotional release valve, but of course you know that, being a doctor and all."

Dud doctored his coffee and took a sip.

"Right?"

"Oh …" said Doc, "right … of course. We took Epithets 1A and 1B in medical school, naturally. 'Emotional release valves and their perfection' they were called. I got an A in Epithetology for the Masses in my third year, too."

"You're just putting me on."

"Maybe."

"Let's look for a moment," chimed in Bert, "at why epithets are so good for the soul."

"He's going to wave his arms again," whispered Doc to Dud.

"I'm afraid so…"

"Yes," said Bert, waving his arms, "epithets, particularly those where no swearing is involved, are like a frustrated man's crossword puzzle. They bring out enough cleverness and creativity in a man to pour salve on whatever it is that's bugging the bejeesus out of him."

"I know I feel better with salve poured on my bejeesus," said Doc, nodding.

"First thing I do in the morning, after coffee," said Dud.

"Well, here comes Steve," Doc said, as all eyes turned to the cowboy who looked wise, in the way a caffeine-starved owl looks wise. "He'll pour some salve and sense on this entire situation.

"Mornin' Steve," said Dud. "What's going on?"

"Bilious blasphemers, it's hot today!" said Steve.

The groaning continued, off and on, through the toast course.

Dud was in a quandary. It was all about Randy Jones and Katie Burchell. There was something so ... *exquisite* about them finding each other and walking around town holdings hands. Exquisite, that was the word.

Dud Campbell pulled the tiny notebook out of his back pocket and wrote down: "Randy and Katie, exquisite."

He'd read this story about writing where it said you should keep a notebook and jot down an idea when it hit you. That way, you won't have to wonder, "What was that word I had that described Randy and Katie walking around town holding hands." And, the story said, you don't worry about a plot, but you just keep making notes. Make notes and when you fill one book, put it in a drawer and start on another. Before you know it, a plot will come along, and you'll be ready to write it.

Dud loved reading these stories, because he knew if he just followed their suggestions, his murder mystery about the duchess and the truck driver will eventually take care of itself. If he just had some insight on what happened between Randy and Katie, he'd be able to do a flashback thingie to let his readers know how a duchess and a truck driver found happiness in each other's arms. On the surface, a truck driver and a duchess don't seem to have a lot in common, but he'd been working on that, too. He had several ideas jotted down in the notebook: books they enjoyed reading, watching old movies on television, polka dancing. He wasn't sure that duchesses liked polka dancing, but he was pretty sure truck drivers didn't like waltzes, and that's all you saw duchesses doing.

Dud had some time, so he followed the young couple from a block away, hoping his keen senses would discern the hidden secret to this relationship. He saw them smile on small children and butterflies, their smiles beaming a benediction and blessing on all they met, as though they were pilgrims on a quest for eternal secrets.

Hey, that was pretty good. He whipped out the notebook again and leaned against a mailbox to write it down.

Willoughby breezed through the valley the other day. He lives in the capital city, but whips on through here about once a month, and each time he comes he has new things to sell.

"You suppose," said Bert, watching Willoughby's van pull into town, "he sells all of it each time and fills everyone's orders, or just doesn't sell any of it and has to try new things?"

If we were to ask him, of course, it would ruin the speculation, which is one of the favorite things we do around here. Willoughby, despite his advancing years, leaped out of the van and went into the Soup 'R Market to see Annette. Naturally, we followed.

"Say," Doc said, as we crossed the street, "wasn't Willoughby's hair brown the last time he was here? It's black today."

"I believe you're right," Bert said.

Coal black. We could see that as we came in and bought sodas. Shoe polish, I think.

We settled back against the pop machine and prepared to enjoy the show.

"Whatcha got, Willoughby?"

"The latest and greatest thing going, Annette. You know how you can't get fresh seafood here because of the distance, right? Well, now there's Simulated brand Seafood, all the flavor of the briny deep without any of the delicacy that makes it go bad on you."

"Simulated?"

"Just as good as the real thing. Yes, ma'am, I have simulated swordfish steaks, slightly sea bass, faux flounder, kinda crab, and our number one seller this week … you ready for this … tah DAH …. Scarcely Scallops!"

"I don't know, Willoughby…"

He sparkled right up to the challenge. We sipped on those pops. This beat anything on TV.

"Now we have simulated seafood, with a shelf life that will keep all your customers happy for as long as they want to hang onto them."

Annette said no to Willoughby, sending him on down the road to greener pastures. It's just as well. I'm holding out for Prit-Near Prawns myself.

The sign in front of the gas station says "Unleaded, 2.39, special on Colt .357 Magnum, six-inch barrel."

Visitors to our valley do a double take when they see Vince's sign there at what we all now know as "the gas station gun shop." That's because Vince doesn't believe in being deprived of his passion while earning a living. His passion: guns. His living: pumping gas.

We had all known of his passion for many years. He is the perennial president of the local rod and gun club, plans nearly all their annual spaghetti feeds to raise money for targets. If you want to go hunting, all you need to do is pull up in front of Vince's house on the edge of town with some hounds in the back of the truck in the evening and honk the horn. You don't even need to call ahead.

The combination business began about three years ago when an out-of-town customer pulled up to the gas pumps, walked inside to pay Vince, and saw the owner sitting there polishing a 1911 Government Model .45 auto.

CPR wasn't necessary, but it did give Vince some thinking to do.

"I looked around in here," he said, "and saw all this wall space. What did I have on it? Fan belts, stacks of motor oil containers, those little air fresheners shaped like pine trees. What a waste! So I put that stuff out in the repair side of the station and nailed up this knotty pine. Looks pretty good, doesn't it?

"Then I got my federal firearms license, bought a bunch of ammunition and some guns, and set it up."

He says he's always sure to put a gun ad up on the big white sign, along with the gas prices, so people won't be surprised when they walk in and find him cleaning a Model 70 behind the counter.

"I actually do okay in the gun business here," he said. "It isn't enough to be a gun shop on its own, really. We aren't a big enough town."

He grins. "And I've never been held up."

It's not fair that kids have all the summer fun. It's not that we begrudge them the running and squealing and yelling "Help!" when they aren't in trouble. We don't. We look at them and say, "I can remember what that felt like…"

So if you're under 10 years old, go tell your mama she wants you, because this is just for more "experienced" people.

Pssst… It's summer. It's hot. It's …. *sprinkler time!*

Oh yes. Since we're over 10, we'll wear bathing suits … probably, and we more than likely won't want a crowd around, either. But why should just children get to run through the sprinkler? Even if we have to … well, *hobble* through the sprinkler.

The whole idea is to feel once more those diamond drops of cooling paradise caressing our legs and tummies and chests. To feel the cool of the water as it hits us and tells us we're not too old to have fun.

When we were small we ran through whatever kind of sprinkler our parents furnished us. But now we're the ones in charge. Now we can pick and choose the right one.

The venerable Rain Bird? Nope. It irrigates beautifully, but stings legs as it goes chu....chu....chu....chu ....chu-chu-chu-chu back to home base again. What we need is something soft and soothing, and the old-fashioned one-piece flower-blossom sprinkler that sits there quietly and radiates is just the ticket.

Now there is always the chance of offspring witnessing this and applying to the state for full custody of your pickup and their choice of rest home if you're caught. So here's the plan.

Do this at night! After all, we're old enough to be out after dark now, right? And our lawns absorb more water after dark anyway. And should a grandkid or two catch us and ask why we're wearing a bathing suit?

"There's always the remote chance," you tell them, "with these primitive water-distribution devices, to end up with wet clothing. This is simply my way of saving on a potential cleaning bill."

Hey, it *might* work....

Herb Collins may be forgiven for his fake lawn. We all know about the knee surgery he had, and how difficult it's been for him to get around since then. He had to pay neighborhood kids to mow the lawn for him, and his wife had to water it, something neither of them wanted to happen. Herb was always afraid she'd miss spots with the spray from the nozzle and cause yellow blotches.

But life doesn't always deal us a fair hand, so Herb was forced to sit in the living room and worry about his lawn. The kids didn't edge it right, either. There was definite intrusion into the bulb bed and the pansy patch.

Just what caused him to put in fake lawn is still a matter of conjecture. Some like the "his wife made him do it so she doesn't have to water any more" theory, while others believe Herb just didn't want to be bothered with all the work a lawn entails.

We watched the truck come that day, and the sod that held some 40 years of Herb's labors was taken up and rolled into green-looking sleeping bags and placed on a flat bed truck. Then the fake lawn came and was rolled into place. Green, cut forever short and even. Never will it encroach on pansies or tulips. It went down smoothly and looked exactly alike in every square foot, appearing to be more like indoor/outdoor carpet than anything else.

When it was in and done, it was forever in and it was forever done. No watering, no fertilizing, no mowing, no edging. If you dug the snow off it in winter, it would be as green as it is now. Forever. No dandelions. No crabgrass. No nutgrass. Nothing to pull.

But a lawn can sometimes mean something to a guy. For most of us, it's as close as we're ever likely to get to a farm. But we can grow it, and patch it, and water it, and fertilize it, and discuss its care endlessly. It makes up for not having 200 acres of sorghum or wheat.

Looking at your lawn isn't really something a fellow does a lot. It's just one of those things we do when we need to grow things. When we need to be outside and scratching our agricultural itch.

Herb doesn't have to sweat in the summer sun any more, mowing grass when he could be inside watching a game. He's got it made now. That's why we kinda wonder when he comes over to visit, hobbling a bit with that cane, when we're out working on our lawns.

All Jim wanted was a cup of coffee when he stopped down at the Mule Barn the other day. Sometimes when he comes the three miles down off the interstate with his big rig he has a full meal, but this afternoon it was just for a quick cup and a friendly smile.

He got the friendly smile from Mavis, but she forgot the coffee until the second time she asked him what he wanted. It was embarrassing for her, but Jim just smiled. He left her a five-dollar tip for the 85-cent coffee, too. More and more of the old-time truckers do that these days. The first thing they do is ask which tables Mavis is waiting on, and they are sure to sit there and leave a big tip.

Mavis has raised her three kids alone now for several years, and things haven't always been easy for her, but she always has something nice to say to everyone. She's not as quick as she was years ago. Sometimes a guy has to sit there and jaw with his pals for a while before he gets his order, but that's okay. She sometimes forgets to hold the onions on a burger, too, but no one complains. It's not hard to take the onions off a burger and set them to one side if you don't want them.

81

Sometimes she forgets when someone wants decaf instead of regular, too. I've seen one of the other girls quietly wait until Mavis was in the kitchen and then go take care of it.

It's no crime to be a little forgetful when you have more important things on your mind. Mavis wears a scarf on her head these days, but that's just temporary, too. Her hair will grow back after she's finished with the treatments.

The word got around, as it does in these small communities of ours. It was to be Tuesday. Tuesday evening. He said he'd pick her up at seven.

Those of us closely following the Randy Jones/Katie Burchell celebration of life and love were excited about this. The holding hands and walking around town in a state of bliss and benediction had escalated. Somehow or other, Randy had asked Katie on a real date.

And she'd told her mother and her mother told Mrs. Greer, and Mrs. Greer lived next door to Olivia, who cooks at the Mule Barn, and Olivia told Loretta the waitress, and by that time, it might as well have been on the Channel Four news.

Randy and Katie were coming to the Mule Barn for dinner on Tuesday. Shortly after seven. It would take them a few minutes to walk over there, hand-in-hand, and then?

Well, that's what the topic of discussion was Tuesday morning among the members of the world dilemma think tank. They all agreed it was time to take their wives out for dinner, maybe at the Mule Barn? Sevenish?

So in came the two shy teenage love birds at 7:10 p.m., and there sat the Supreme Court of Everything That Goes On In Our Valley, sitting there with their wives, and everyone was smiling. The kids looked self conscious for a minute, but then Katie found them a booth and they both sat on the same side so they could hold hands.

Then here came Loretta, with a checkered tablecloth she'd brought from home. And Olivia came out of the kitchen with a candle in an empty wine bottle. Doc got up and found some Johnny Mathis snuggle music on the juke box, and Dud unscrewed two light bulbs in their portion of the dining room. For atmosphere. It was romantic enough to hug a cactus. A night to remember.

82 Oh … and Randy and Katie enjoyed it, too.

Ol' Flint rode into town the other day, sitting tall and straight behind the wheel of his battered old pickup. Behind him was the horse trailer that doubles as his home, and his faithful horse, Rodeo Clown, was looking out over the edge of it as they pulled up to the Mule Barn truck stop.

Now Ol' Flint is not his real name, but is the cowboy name he adopted when he moved to this country from England years ago and became what he calls "The Last Great American Cowboy." Oh, he looks like one. Hat, boots, mustache, everything Western. It's only when he opens his mouth to say something that you realize he ain't really from around here.

He sounds like Eliza Doolittle's father.

But Flint is a part of the pattern of life around here and we think he's an OK guy. His life consists largely of riding around on his horse. He rides hundreds of miles on his horse and he lives in the horse trailer. The front end of it has a tiny apartment. He was arrested once for riding his horse into Tombstone, Arizona, because he was also packing a six shooter.

"Can you imagine?" he said, indignantly, "you can't carry a six shooter in Tombstone? Disgusting, innit? A tragedy. A Western tragedy."

One of his favorite things during summer, when the tourists come, is to ride down to the town square and pose like a statue of General Grant for the clicking of Instamatics. He looks the part of the cowboy until he speaks.

"I were down there t'other day," he says, "and there were these two women, nice and plump they was, too, and they took pictures of us and they says to each other, 'What a magnificent beast' and I smiles back at 'em, y'know, and I says, "Thank you, misses, and my horse is good looking, too."

Dud and Anita Campbell were driving home from the store when they saw the two horses ahead, walking patiently, side-by-side, so their riders, Katie Burchell and Randall Jones, could hold hands. Dud reached over and took his wife's hand and they smiled.

It hit him a block later. Like a thunderstorm that sweeps over the horizon. Like a tsunami, or at least like Dud thought a tsunami would be like, overpowering. He sped home and ran into the house, forgetting to help Anita with the groceries.

Anita heard the typing going on in the next room, and brought her husband a cup of coffee. She had a peek over his shoulder. Oh yes, it was the duchess and the truck driver again.

The duchess looked up from her cup of coffee at the truck stop in Budapest, he had written, *and there he stood, like a knight of old, holding his trucking coffee mug, and with a copy of the local paper under his arm. She had no way of knowing, right then, that he couldn't read the paper, being an American trucker on special assignment, but he liked to look at the cartoons.*

"Is this seat taken?" he asked.

"Why, no," she replied, lowering her pince nez, so she could see him better. "Won't you join me?"

"Aah," thought the trucker, 'she speaks English. She's probably not from around here.'"

But he was wrong on that. How did he have any way of knowing that she came from that castle up on the hill outside of town. He'd noticed that when he hit the jake brakes coming down the incline, sending rabbits and red stags scurrying for cover. If he'd known then what was coming, the murders, the child of their love, how cold that castle was in winter, would he have sat down with the duchess? Who knows?

Dud looked up at Anita and smiled. She handed him the coffee. "Back on track with the duchess?" she asked.

"*And* the truck driver," he said. "And the truck driver."

When old Ben died recently, the town was saddened, but not just for the usual reasons. Ben had been widowed for nearly 20 years and had lived alone in the house where he and Judith had raised their boy, John.

Ben had a lot of health problems, there at the last, too. Things weren't easy for him.

Sometimes when a guy is in that shape, people nod and smile slightly at his passing and say, "Well, in a way it's a blessing, isn't it."

But not with old Ben. There's the sailboat, you see.

After Judith died – and Judith was the most practical woman in town – Ben started buying and reading magazines about sailboats. Then he cut the front off the barn/garage out in back, and began building one. He drew crowds with his work for a while. Everyone stopped by from time to time, and we all know it is to be 32 feet long and a gaff-rigged – not Marconi-rigged – sloop. Said they look more like real sailboats.

Eccentric? Well, maybe. Eccentricities last a year or two, but a 20-year project is a lot closer to being an obsession.

When Ben could afford more of the special wood he was using, he bought it. Sometimes all he'd get were some of those little brass whatchits to put along the side. But each time something came, there was work going on out in that garage. Ben took pride in the project being pay-as-you-go, so he wouldn't owe anybody when he finally put it in the ocean.

Ben died before that happened, and that saddened us greatly. We might chuckle a bit behind his back, but we also secretly envied him and admired him for building that boat.

After Ben passed, his son John brought his wife and children to live in the little house. After a few weeks, we heard activity out in the garage, and we found John working on his dad's boat. It would, he said, eventually sail.

There is no statute of limitations on dreams.

As we get older, we don't go to the swimming hole on Lewis Creek as often as we used to, and it's a shame.

A recent jaunt down there brought a reminder of what we'd been missing, and slapped us with a lifetime of happy memories of splashing diamonds in the August sun.

There is something about the swimming hole, heat, green leaves on the surrounding trees and children's laughter that go together. Throw in the barking of two or three ecstatic dogs and the smell of burgers cooking, and the result is a symphony of life itself.

Even sitting in the shade on folding chairs is a thrill these days. Oh, we remember when our dads put that swinging rope up on the cottonwood limb after the old one broke. The old one was one used by their parents when they were kids. We'll have to check this one to see how much life it has left in it. Maybe we don't swing out and drop in the water with arms and legs flailing against the blue universe the way we used to. Not any more. But there's nothing wrong with our memories and we can remember how it felt to swing out and up and let go and fly and hang suspended for one delicious split second of immortality before plunging into the deep hole and the cool water beneath us.

Every time a youngster swings out now, we watch and in a way it's us doing it, too. We can feel the rough whiskers on the rope, fill our lungs as the youngster does at the very apogee of the swing, feel the water cool our bodies in summer bliss as we drop down to the bottom and push off the rocks with our bare feet and rise to the surface.

We can feel it each summer, and for summer after summer until our memories fail or we don't make it back here. But on a day like this one, a guy tends to make private plans to live forever.

"Isn't that a beautiful picture," Marvin Pincus said. His wife, Marjorie, stirred her coffee and agreed. Outside their home, there went Randall Jones and Katie Burchell, walking by hand-in-hand and looking adoringly at each other.

"What I did for Randy," Marvin said, "I think I should do for others. What do you think, Hon?"

Marjorie nodded. Marjorie had been nodding for nearly 50 years now. What Marvin had done for Randy amounted to tying two fishing flies while Randy sat there trying to figure out why Mr. Pincus had sent for him, and listening to Marvin tell him that good fish were attracted to plain, honest flies and not flashy stuff. This was to turn Randy's head away from the fabulously shallow (but slightly gorgeous) Marcia Fleming. The lesson must've taken, because the next thing you knew, Randy and Katie were a town item. Marvin didn't know it was Katie being what old people would call "forward" that turned the tide, and he thought he might have something to contribute in fly-tying therapy.

"I thought we could use my den, Dear. Would that be all right with you?"

Marjorie looked up. "Use your den for what, Sweetie?"

"My counseling service. You know, I have the fly-tying bench already set up there, and maybe we could just get a more comfortable chair for the patient to sit in while we talk."

"But you don't have the education..."

"Hey ... school of hard knocks, a successful marriage, and sixty years of tying flies. Sounds like a good education to me. Let's go shopping for a chair this afternoon, okay?"

Marjorie smiled at the husband she had who would never really get old.

"Sure. Why not? I think something green would be nice."

"And it has to be comfortable, too," he said, grinning.

Sometimes there's a feeling in the early evening air that makes you know this is a special time. The planets line up, the fish spawn, the squirrels ... well, do their squirrel-type stuff. Magic. And that's what Katie Burchell was feeling as she held Randy Jones's hand as they made their daily walk through our town.

"Randy?"

"Yes?"

"Are you happy having me for your girlfriend?"

"Oh yes. I think you're ... *wonderful!*"

"Maybe we should take our relationship to ... a new level?"

"You mean ..."

"I think we should kiss each other."

Randy was silent and looked at shade trees.

"You don't want to?" Katie asked.

"Oh, *yes*. It's just ..." He stopped and looked at her. "I've ... never kissed a girl before."

"No problem. We'll get it done. Only thing is, to be proper, I think you should ask me first, okay?"

"Uh, sure. Katie, would ... may I kiss you?"

"Yes. But not here. I'll show you."

So they continued walking until they stood right in front of Marcia Fleming's house. Marcia the Magnificent, Princess of Teenage Dreams. Former princess of Randy's dreams.

"This looks like a good spot," Katie said, smiling. "So just close your eyes."

He did, and it happened, and planets went swirling into space and squirrels took a coffee break and a new world began. And they smiled at each other. Then Katie looked at the house and smiled at the face peering out the window.

As the bumper sticker says: *Love your neighbors but brand your calves.*

Dewey's a community project.

Quite a few of us have scratched our heads over helping Dewey find something he could do without causing widespread destruction.

Last year, Dewey fixed up his dad's pickup and became what Doc later called an "entre-manure," by taking manure from feedlots and the dairy and delivering it as fertilizer to people's gardens. The problem is, no one needs fertilizer in their gardens in winter.

Bert, who keeps up on these things, suggested that Dewey look into vermiculture. He explained that this was *not* a new dish at the Italian restaurant, but rather the raising of worms and the creation of compost.

"It's a win-win deal, Dewey," Bert said. "You put the worms in the manure. They multiply and replenish the earth, then they leave behind rich compost. You can get more money for composted manure next spring than the raw stuff, and you'll have worms to sell to fishermen."

Dewey went out the door so fast he forgot to pay for his coffee, so we got it.

A few weeks later, Dewey was as happy as a chairman of the board of something wonderful.

He discovered that worms don't eat and reproduce as readily when they're cold, so to speed up the project, he built some worm crates, filled them with worms and manure, and spread them around. As I said, he's a community project. He has two worm bins in Steve's spare room, three in Doc's garage, two in his mother's garage, and two in the basement first-grade classroom at Pastor Jeff's Sunday school, because Sunday school just happens not to have any first graders this year.

Haven't seen Bert around lately, though. We've been looking for him, too.

When Jim Kennedy uses his big backhoe, a crowd usually gathers. He's an artist.

He runs his massive-toothed monster gouging holes in the backyards of his neighbors, putting in their pipes and even the occasional swimming pool, and does it with the grace of a surgeon.

At Bud McFarland's place the other day, he was there to install Bud's new septic tank. This was to be a massive septic tank, Bud said, "big enough so if I want to put in a hotel, I don't have to worry."

It was a balmy day, past coffee time, and the backhoe master was at work. Bud was standing there watching Jim work his digging magic in the backyard, along with half a dozen others, including us. Now and then Jim would just do something to show off his skill. At one point, when Jim's backhoe cut through a buried tree root, there was about a foot-long section of root lying alone at the bottom of the hole.

"Hey," Bud yelled at Jim, good-naturedly, "firewood!"

Jim grinned and reached his long steel arm down into the hole, gently picking up just the one piece of wood, lifting it out of the hole, and delivering it to Bud's outstretched hand as though it were the crown jewels.

As we watched, Jim lifted the massive concrete vault of the septic tank and placed it gently in the hole. Then his helper hooked a chain to the septic tank lid and Jim lifted this into the air and swung it over the hole. But instead of lowering it, Jim stopped the machine in mid stride and hollered at the new septic tank owner.

"Hey Bud!" he yelled, "Got any bodies you want to hide?"

The perfect place for a murder victim. Agatha Christie didn't even come up with that one.

You have to admire professionalism wherever you find it.

Marvin Pincus paced up and down the house and in the yard and drove Marjorie crazy until the local paper hit the lawn. The Valley Weekly Miracle was like many other local American papers; it's what people can't wait to read to see how much the editor dared to print.

With the paper spread out on the kitchen table, Marvin quickly found his ad under "Local Services."

Try the fly-tying method of achieving success in life and love. Is your love life a catch-and-release situation? From the slightest midge of problems to the deepest wire-wrapped bead-head wooly bugger dilemmas, let the master fly tier and advice giver help you cast out your troubles and make your dreams come true. Proven results! Call Marvin Pincus. (and gave his phone number).

He grinned while reading it at least four times, and then handed it to Marjorie.

"What do you think, Honey?"

"Proven results?" she said.

"Hey, Randy and Katie. The proof is in the pudding. All we have to do now is wait for the phone to ring. We've got the new chair set up in the den and I've got all the fly-tying ingredients ready. I even picked up more goose biots in case someone has a stonefly nymph complication. They work well on the feelers and the split tails, you know. They'll get right to the bottom of the creek … and the problems."

"Well … it's sure good to see you enjoying this. Are you sure you're ready?"

He thought a minute. "To be honest, I'm a bit weak on those swept-back wings on the wet flies. Need a lot more practice with those, but for the dry fly problems, my hackles will stand up to anyone's."

Marjorie smiled at her husband of so many years.

"I'm sure they will, Marvin. I'm sure they will."

Steve was out in the Mule Barn parking lot the other day, tightening something with his wrenches under the hood of his pickup truck. The rest of us stood around, looking wise, and sipping coffee.

"You sure it ain't the solenoid?" said Bert.

"I don't think they make them anymore," said Doc.

"It's usually the solenoid," Bert said, with finality.

Out of self defense, Steve emerged from his cavern of wires and metal long enough to say, "Didn't I see you have a goat now, Bert?"

Bert nodded. "That's why I hate allergies."

We waited. We stared.

"Well, you see, Maizie's allergic to cow's milk, so we bought Ernestine for her."

"And Ernestine is ….?"

"The goat … right. So what happens is somehow I have to milk Ernestine. Twice a day. We wanted to go overnight to the city last week. Ever try to find someone who will babysit and milk a goat?"

"I won't do it," said Dud.

"Neither will anyone else," said Bert, sadly. "So we either stay home, or take the goat with us. Ever try to find a motel that takes goats?"

"Not recently," Doc said.

"So we stayed home. Oh, it wouldn't be so bad if she liked me…"

"Maizie?"

"Ernestine. See, she waits until I have her almost milked out, then she'll stick her foot in the bucket and kick it all over me. The other day, I was standing in her pen and talking with Mrs. Gonzales next door, and Ernestine came running up behind me and ran right between my legs."

"Did you fall?"

"Of course. And Mrs. Gonzales tried not to laugh, but it didn't work."

"Bert," said Doc, "why don't you just buy goat's milk at the store?"

"Maizie says she needs it fresh, because it's better. You guys ever notice how a goat has horns and cloven hooves?"

We nodded.

"I don't think I need to add anything to that," said Bert.

By the time we sat and flipped our cups to fillable positions at the Mule Barn truck stop, Dewey was already there and having breakfast. It's always such a treat to see Dewey, because that means he's still alive and hasn't had another wreck and gone the way of the passenger pigeon.

"Hi guys!" he said.

"Hey, Dewey," said Steve. "How's it going with the business?"

"Never better, Steve. I can't thank you guys enough for getting me started in it."

Steve had once suggested that what this accident-prone good guy needed was a job that dealt in a product that was worth exactly nothing in case it got Dewey'd by mistake. So Dewey began shoveling cow manure at the dairy and selling it as fertilizer to folks who have gardens in town.

"I hear you've gone into worms, too," Doc said.

"Oh yeah. I got some from Bert's worm bin and started my own. The worm castings sell for more than the fertilizer, and I've started selling worms to the kids for a buck a quart to use for fishing."

We looked at each other and nodded.

"Then I talked them into paying me something each month to shovel manure out at the dairy, so not only is it free, I get paid a little something to go get it. In fact, I made enough money I put a dump bed on the pickup truck."

"No kidding?"

"Saves me having to shovel the truck out. Works really good, too. Not counting the accident."

Doc looked alarmed. "Accident?"

"Yeah. Just dumped a load and set my lunch box down behind the cab. When I lowered the bed, it crushed right through two tuna sandwiches and a new Thermos bottle."

It's comforting to know there are things you can count on in this world.

⌒⌒

"Now *that's* the job I want," said Steve, putting down the paper. "A guy could really sink his teeth into something like that."

Doc looked up from his coffee. "Didn't know you were looking for work, Steve. Cowboying not working out for you?"

"It isn't that," said the cowboy/farrier, "it's just that a guy should always keep his eyes open so as not to miss an opportunity to better himself. That's why I'm so interested in becoming a chicken ranger."

"A what?"

"He said a chicken ranger, Doc," said Bert, "but I never heard of one."

"Scoff if you must, friends," said Steve with a flourish, "but right here in the pages of our own glorious newspaper, the Valley Weekly Miracle, comes one of the best ideas for a job I've ever heard of. It seems if your chickens run around loose, you get more money for their eggs. No. Seriously. Look at this ad. The store says they are from certified free-ranging chickens. Got it stamped right on every free-ranging egg."

"Heard about that," Doc said, nodding. "It's not that the eggs are better, but it makes you feel better about eating an egg from a happy hen, 'cause she can run around and peck on other hens and get pecked on rather than be caged."

"And therein lies my new job, gentlemen," Steve said. "Someone has to make sure those are happy, unfettered, free-ranging manufacturers of cackleberries, and I'm just the guy to get 'er done."

Bert, who takes his charter membership in the Mule Barn truck stop's philosophy counter and world dilemma think tank very seriously, said, "Doesn't sound like much work to me."

"Each egg has to be certified," Steve explained. "Gotta be a chicken ranger there to certify those hens didn't bunch up in a corner somewhere, right? So I'll be sitting there on my horse, keeping an eye on the girls…"

"On your horse?"

"Of course," Steve said. "If you can't do a job horseback it ain't worth doing. Don't you know *afoot* are the two saddest words in the English language?"

It happened in the checkout lane down at the Soup 'R' Market last week. We discussed it thoroughly, of course, and no one knows yet what to make of it.

As sometimes happens, when we are glancing at the tabloids to see who fathered Bigfoot's new baby, we get into discussions of trivia. Annette was sliding broccoli and corn flakes over the glass-window dinger machine, and we were just chatting about … I think it was bears this time. You know…

"I read," said Annette, "that a bear can run 45 miles an hour, faster than a race horse."

To which I added, "Did you know a polar bear's skin is black, and a black bear's skin is white?"

"Really?" Annette said, weighing the plastic bag of apples. "And did you know," she said, "that horses can't vomit?"

Horses just hadn't heard me sing yet, that's all.

So it was then that the next guy in line, a young fellow dressed in camouflage, smiled and joined in.

"You know the song, 'The Duke of Earl'?" he asked.

Well, of course we did. We used to slide around the dance floor to that when Elvis was still a pup. Wasn't as good for snuggling as a Johnny Mathis tune, but what is? Half the marriages in this town began while dancing to "The Twelfth of Never."

"Well, here's something to think about," our young friend said. "If you are driving down the highway, and you tap your foot on the accelerator each time the car goes by one of those broken yellow lines, and if you do it in time to 'The Duke of Earl,' you're doing exactly 55 miles an hour."

"You're kidding!"

"Nope. I'm a trucker, and I can tell you it's a fact. Heard it on the radio and gave it a try. Fifty-five miles an hour."

Let's see … Duke, duke, duke, duke of earl, duke, duke, duke of earl, duke…

Might come in handy if the speedometer goes on the fritz.

Marjorie Pincus looked out the front window at her husband, Marvin, and smiled. No matter how old he gets, she thought, he'll always be the boy I remember, riding his bicycle through this town so many years ago.

Marvin had stopped picking out the nutgrass and was watching a small group of children across the street in the park. Two of them had kites, and the brisk wind of morning had them both up as high as string would allow. Soon, Marvin had ambled across the street and was standing behind the children, watching the taut dip in the string and listening to the rattle of the tight paper.

The first time Marvin Pincus flew a kite in this park, airplanes didn't go very far or very fast. The other side of the moon was a mystery in those days, and no one really thought man would ever go there and back. Not really.

And here these kids are, flying their kites the very same way, with the very same rag tails, and looking up at the earth-tied fliers climbing with the gusts and settling with the relaxation of the breezes.

Marjorie watched from across the street as the Herrera boy walked over to Marvin, whispering something as Marvin leaned down to hear, and then handed the stick with the kite string tied to it to the old man. His face beamed as he controlled flight once again. The kids smiled, too, probably not realizing kite flying was the same when Mr. Pincus was a kid, too.

But what about the dreams? Marjorie thought about this. What goes through the minds of today's kite fliers who know what the surface of Mars looks like, who know what the far side of the moon looks like, who know there are human beings in a space station, living up there, right now? What will their dreams be as the kites dance?

What dreams will dance now as they stand there and hold the miracle of flight in their fingers?

When, in the course of rural events, it becomes necessary to straighten out the world situation, invent a new gadget, or provide for the common fishing good, there are two venues: coffee or the hunker.

94

It struck Dud Campbell out at the sales barn the other day. No coffee, therefore no choice. All the signs were there. He turned quiet and he started checking the weed margins for a grass blade.

In a hunker, two props are necessary: a stick and a blade of grass. Oh, sometimes straw is substituted, but it's kinda like trading your French fries for cottage cheese on the lunch special: they'll do it, but it isn't the same.

Dud found a good stick, finger thick, about a foot long. Cottonwood, maybe. Then he found a tall blade of orchard grass, broke it until it was hunker length, and stuck it in his mouth. Doc and I, having witnessed these events, began looking for our own grass blades, albeit reluctantly. Our knees aren't as young as Dud's.

That's when Dud went headlong into Phase Three. Grass... check. Stick ... ten-four. Phase Three, the right location.

Dud began turning slowly, checking the ground beneath his feet, lining up with the azimuth in just the right way so as to maximize his powers, keeping the sun in the proper location to light his face while not causing his own eyes to squint. Slowly he turned, like a mare about to choose her foaling bed, then a silent string was pulled in Dud's mind, releasing the knees, and he dropped down into a proper country hunker.

Doc and I stuck our grass between our teeth and - with occasional moans - followed suit.

Dud silently brushed a clean slate of dirt in front of him and doodled on it.

"Been thinking," he said.

Doc and I nodded and checked the doodle to see if we could recognize anything about the design. Nope.

"I think," Dud said, "if we would just irrigate more, we'd get more rain."

Doc isn't even sure why he did it. For days afterwards, people would talk about it, then smile and shake their heads and just say "Oh, that *Doc...*"

The whole thing came up on the spur of the moment. Doc and Mrs. Doc were planning to go out of town for a few days and needed several hundred dollars in cash, so Doc dropped by the bank to take it out.

He drew Ardis Richardson as his teller, after he wound his way through the bank's roped rat maze, and told her how much he needed.

Then, on an impulse, he leaned forward and whispered, "Ardis, I need that in small, unmarked bills, please."

"Unmarked, Doc?"

"My squirrel's life depends on it."

Ardis's mouth dropped open. That should have stopped Doc, but it didn't.

"They said if I wanted to see him alive again, the bills would have to be unmarked."

She stared.

"Have you ever seen how cute he is when he sits up and eats a nut and his whiskers twitch? I mean, right now I can picture his big fluffy tail and those eyes … those eyes…. Oh my…"

"Doc … I didn't know," she said.

He nodded sadly. "I can hardly bear looking at his little squirrel bed, sitting there empty, and his squirrel food dish, with only half his meal gone. I really have no choice."

Ardis gave him the money. The sheriff came by Doc's office to make sure everything was all right. Mrs. Miller across the street from Steve's house sent a five dollar donation to Doc to help rescue the squirrel. Pop Walker down at the Rest of Your Life home volunteered to get his gun and polish off every squirrel-napper in the county.

Doc, you see, doesn't have a squirrel. Never did.

Mrs. Doc thought this weekend away from home came at just about the right time.

The morning conference began innocently enough, with Steve and Doc arguing over which of the little packaged jellies went better on sourdough toast, and no one caring which one was right.

Dud and Bert and I sat silently, sucking down the morning elixir until it spread life to our outermost reaches as the Mule Barn truck stop's world dilemma think tank crept to life. Bert was unusually quiet this morning and we asked why. He hemmed and hawed a little, then said, "Doc, you know about these things. What exactly is female trouble?"

Oh shoot. Pretty heavy stuff for just two cups of coffee, so the rest of us hurried down a third as Doc puffed up a bit and got ready.

"Sure, Bert," Doc said kindly. Then Doc gave us the best his nine years of college and 50 years of medical practice had blessed him with. He waxed eloquent on hormonal elements, the ebb and flow of female fertility, things that could go wrong with tubular parts, and the effect all of these things could have on the attitudinal proclivities of the dear ladies we all love and admire. He took a break while Loretta returned with more coffee and with strange looks at our faces while we tried not to stare at her.

Then she was gone, and Doc began again. Finally, when we had been pretty well checked out on the mysterious workings of the gentle gender, Doc said, "Bert, if Maizie is having some problems, have her give me a call."

"Oh, it ain't *her*, Doc," Bert said. "It's Dud."

We all looked at Dud. He grinned sheepishly. No one wanted to say anything. Finally, Steve said, "I'm not going to be the one to ask."

"That's what you said, Dud, right?" Bert asked. "That's why Saturday's plans are shot."

"*Female* trouble?" Doc said, looking at his old friend.

Dud nodded. "Anita won't let me go fishing this weekend."

It was Dewey who rang Marvin Pincus's doorbell. Dewey of the multiple "fatalities." Dewey the accident prone. Dewey who tied his horse to a bee tree. Dewey who managed to turn 60 head of cattle onto the freeway.

He told Marvin he was there for the counseling and had saved up some money from his fertilizer delivery service, and needed some help. Marvin delightedly showed Dewey into the fly-tying room and saw that he was comfortably settled in the new green "client's" chair. Marjorie made a pot of coffee and brought a cup of it for Dewey and some tea for Marvin. Then she quietly closed the door so they could have privacy.

"So Dewey," Marvin said, "what can I help you with today?"

"I heard you can tie flies and help people with their love lives, Marvin."

Marvin nodded, basking in his Randy/Katie-results fame.

"You might have heard that I sometimes have … well, *accidents*. I think that may hurt my love life."

"In what way, Dewey?"

"I don't have one."

Marvin reached into his drawer and took out a number 6 hook and began wrapping it with lead wire.

"For this we'll need to go deep into your past, Dewey, so I'm tying you a wooly bugger with a lead-wire wrap to dive down to the seat of your problems. See the fly getting heavier and heavier? Let it take you back … back … back. Now, when did you first notice your love life suffering?"

"Right after I began hauling cow manure into town for gardeners."

Marvin stopped his green chenille in mid wrap, flipped up his magnifying lenses and looked closely at Dewey. He also used his olfactory senses.

"Dewey," Marvin said, choosing his words carefully, "before you ask a girl out … do you *shower?*"

Janice Thomas came in the Mule Barn for breakfast the other day, and sat at the counter for the first time. She usually gets one of the tables, or a booth against the wall. We were kinda flattered that she'd come sit with us, but wondered why. After all, this high school art teacher never has been one to sit down and solve the world's problems, the way we do.

She didn't keep us waiting long, though.

"Boys," she said, "I have a deer pointer."

She let the silence pounce heavily on our sweet rolls while we pondered this.

"A what?" Doc said.

"A deer pointer. You want deer, you just let ol' Woof out and you'll find 'em."

"Woof, eh?"

"Yes. He's that new dog I got after that Lab of mine died. I've had Woof for about six months now. He's half bird dog and half heeler and he points deer."

We looked at each other and grinned. When it comes to telling stories at this particular lunch counter, the first liar doesn't stand a chance.

"Points 'em you say?"

"Locks right up. Steady to wing and shot."

"This I have to see," Dud said.

So after coffee we all went out to Janice's place while she turned this little dog out into the wood lot. He ran here and there and then froze into a perfect field-trial point. We walked up quietly and sure enough, there was a doe standing about 40 yards away. We'd never seen anything like it.

"When I got him," Janice explained, "he thought he'd herd deer, with that sheep dog blood he has in him. Well, the first time he tried that, some doe just kicked the puddin' out of him. His tail didn't work right for a week.

"So now he's switched over to the other half of his heritage and points 'em. He's found that works out a lot better for him."

She grinned. "And no … you can't borrow him this fall."

Old Jasper Blankenship came down from the diggin's last week. He always says he has to get groceries, but we believe he comes down three times a year just so he can amaze us with his new philosophies. He gets most of his new philosophies by running an antenna wire up from the cabin to the top of the ridge, and then listening to the radio talk shows.

"Of course you fellas know what anthropology is, right?" Jasper said. "The study of fascinatin' human beings, like me. Heck, I didn't know I was so fascinatin' until that anthopology professor lady came out to the cabin with those graduate students."

"Came up to your cabin?" said Doc.

"Sure did. She called me a rural icon."

"You know, Jasper," Steve said, "maybe if you took a bath more often, people wouldn't call you things like that."

"Go ahead, laugh," he said, chuckling a bit. "She didn't come to your house and call you an icon, did she? Well, these students wanted to know about everything. How I got water, how I made my money, how the woodstove worked, how I could live in a one-room cabin. That one was easy, 'cause you can't live in more than one room at a time, anyway."

"That's true," said Doc, nodding.

"They seemed to be interested in everything. Everything. So I showed them my ax. It's a big old double-bit cruiser that I think my granddaddy had at one time. They wanted to know all about it, so I told them it was the very ax George Washington used to cut down the cherry tree."

"You didn't!"

"Sure did. I don't think they believed me at first, but then I explained that the ax had been through 12 handles and four heads since George had it."

Anita brought Dud some coffee at 9 p.m. and gave her husband a hug. He had two lines typed on a sheet of paper, with the rest of the manuscript sitting beside it.

"How's it going?" she asked.

"Slow right now, Hon."

"It'll come," she said. "You'll see."

Then she left quietly.

Dud Campbell opened the desk drawer and pulled out the title page of the book again. He had typed it up specially, just the way he wanted it, and Anita had put it on the computer.

"Murder in the Soggy Bottoms," it read. "By Dudley M. Campbell."

He smiled.

Of course, the guys down at the Mule Barn truck stop referred to Dud's once-rejected mystery as "The Duchess and the Truck Driver," because the story involves, well, a duchess and a truck driver. After its initial rejection by the publisher, Dud decided to modify it so there would be only three murders in chapter one, rather than the original eight. It has taken some doing, but he plugs away at it when he gets time.

He sipped the coffee and looked out the window at the streetlight shining on the lawn. Do you suppose every artist goes through this? How many mystery writers, Dud thought, face this very same dilemma? For two of the murders, not a problem. But he couldn't decide who murdered number three or why. This seems to be pretty important to the story, so he has to figure it out. Like a puzzle.

He could go with just two murders, he supposed, but that third victim deserved killing, that was the problem. Could he have two murderers? One could knock off the two, the other take care of the third?

Oh well, it's a long, dark night and a good time for thinking, and the coffee's good. And Dud still has his day job, of course. Such things are probably the cornerstones of great creative work.

Several people, including art teacher Janice Thomas, saw Dewey out on his date with that young woman from across the county line. It was at the potluck supper/religious movie in the church basement. Dewey and his date were the youngest people there.

Dewey confided in Reverend Jeff that it was fly-tying love advice from Marvin Pincus that turned the corner in his own quest for romance. He took his wooly bugger from his pocket, with the hook taped for safety, and showed it to him. And Reverend Jeff told Mrs. Abbott in the kitchen, and that was all it took.

Janice learned the secret of Dewey's success within 15 minutes.

"I have a special project for all of you today," Janice told her art class at the high school on Monday morning. "This will be fun as well as creative."

She then explained to them about Marvin's unique fly-tying love advice counseling service, and said, "What we need today is a design for a sign Mr. Pincus can put in his yard. It must incorporate all the elements here, love, advice, and fly tying. All right, let's see what you can come up with."

The class already had heard that Pincus's piscatorial prowess may have played a role in bringing Randy Jones and Katie Burchell together, a rumor begun by Marvin himself, so they nodded.

There was a lot of staring at the ceiling going on and then scribbling, tearing up of paper, and more scribbling. At the end of the hour, it was Jennifer's design that won the day. Janice said she'd take the design to Mr. Pincus and see if he wanted to have a sign made.

Jennifer's sign had a wonderful Adams dry fly with extra-fluffy hackle on the left, and the words, "Fly Tying Love Center." Below it was Marvin's phone number and this note in italics: "Wrap yourself as tightly in love as you are hooked on life itself."

The sign was in Marvin's front yard in just over a week.

There's something to be said for the brightness of day, of course, when the energies of the world improve our lot in life. But for a special time, give me the night. Give me the soft, velvety quiet of a country evening and its own sounds and flavors and scents.

It's good to hear the night shift take over the part of our world we call home. The coyote yaps off in the brush, calling his family to the hunt, the quail have a soft cluck and rustle down by the creek. The crickets set up the background music for all this in a spooky kind of harmony.

It's a resting time for most, but for those who will postpone sleep, there is the secret of another world, where we slow down a little and take a bit more time with our lives. A time when we can hear the world heal a little before it goes back into daily battle again. A time when we can smile and sit and just say thanks for bringing us to another evening like this. If we like, we can do a little mental planning for the next day. Or not.

A country evening is what we get for being good all day.

Dear Olympic Committee:

Dud put the pen down for a minute and checked the spelling. So far so good. He continued.

We watched the boxing at the Olympic Games this summer with great interest and a generous dollop of constern ... anxie... well sir, we worried a bit about those fights. We'd see some guy get pasted in the face and his head would fly backwards and we'd check the scoreboard and the judges wouldn't give the other guy credit for it. Now that's just wrong.

So we've been talking about it, and me and Doc and Steve would like to volunteer to be the judges when you guys do this again in four years. We're even willing to travel over there if you need us. See ... we'll give a guy a point, fair and square, when he hits the other fella. And if both of them come dancing out and circle around each other for the whole round and nobody throws a punch, we'll send them both home and get two guys in there who will mix it up.

Now you're probably wondering if three American judges can be fair. Oh yeah. We talked about it and we don't care if the guy comes from someplace we don't like or can't find on the map. If he fights fair and square, he's okay in our book.

Dud thought a bit and looked out the window at the trees starting to turn color, then returned to the pen.

And just in case you've already hired someone to judge the boxing for next time, we'll be happy to switch events and judge the women's beach volleyball games. We don't know much about them, but all three of us learn fast.

Sincerely,
Dud Campbell

It just happened, you know? One of those serendipitous coincidences that occur when planets line up or you foolishly store oily rags together. It just … happened.

Ardis Richardson was looking through the Soup 'R Market for an egg beater for her mom. Not the electric kind. The turn-the-handle kind. She picked one up and tried it out, causing the friendly little metallic whir that good egg beaters make. What was serendipitous, however, was Anita Campbell not six feet away in the next row thumping pumpkins. As Anita thumped and Ardis whirred, they got in time with each other and Sarah McKinley was checking out kitchen timers and gave one a friendly ding. This got the thumper and whirrer going even more enthusiastically and caused the market's owner, Annette George, to walk over to the three percussionists, grin, and pick up a brand-new stainless steel funnel, purse her lips, and begin to blow a blues tune on it. It was okay, since she owned the store.

Annette, it turns out, played trombone back in high school.

While she was bluesing and Anita was thumping and Sarah was dinging and Ardis was whirring, a kind of blissful harmony began and filled the vegetable aisle with music.

When they finally stopped, and between gales of laughter, Annette said she could put a regular trumpet mouthpiece in the funnel and get a better tone. Anita said not to say anything to her husband, Dud, as he thought his accordion playing was the only music in the family.

They agreed to get together each Wednesday afternoon and practice until they got good enough for a concert.

But they never did.

Serendipity just … happens … in its own good time.

By the time we saw Dud, of course, the damage had been done.

It was Steve who spoke first.

"I don't believe it," the tall cowboy said.

There, on Dud's head, was a sculpture of such blasphemous proportions as would silence all of us in attendance at the Mule Barn truck stop's world dilemma think tank. It was beautiful, of course, but it was also tragic.

"They call it feathered," said Dud, turning red. "A razor cut."

We just stared at the haircut without saying anything. It curved gracefully around his ears, it waved softly in sculptured layers over the top of his head. It fell in gradually decreasing thicknesses down the long back slope of his head toward its tapered termination at the neck.

"It was Anita's idea," Dud said. "She gave me the money for it and everything."

Finally, Doc spoke. "What's Kelly going to say?"

"That's the worst of it, all right," Dud said. "I know he's going to be hurt."

Kelly hadn't really worried too much about the future of his barbershop when Fantasy Fantails set up shop. He assumed it was a haircutting place for women who didn't want to take the time to go to the beauty parlor, and for guys who came to live in our small town from the city.

Kelly's had always been the stronghold of local manhood here. You wouldn't find a single advertisement showing a guy wearing a sweater tied around his neck. Not at Kelly's. In the past, when magazines were magazines, you could read how some guy captured Gestapo headquarters with his headhunter brides.

"Well," said Doc, shrugging. "That haircut of yours is a work of art, without a doubt. But there's at least one good thing about getting a really expensive haircut, Dud. Sooner or later, it'll grow out."

Delbert McLain smiled at the sign in Marvin Pincus's yard as he walked briskly up to the front door and knocked. Marvin had seen him coming and opened it with a big smile and a handshake.

"Delbert! I've got to tell you I've really been looking forward to seeing what kind of flies we can tie up to improve your love life. You want some coffee?"

"Love life?" Del said. "Oh not today, Marvin, not today. I'm here on chamber business. Yessir."

Delbert McLain *is* our Chamber of Commerce. We have all designated him ... well ... okay, I guess Del kinda designated himself to let the world know we adore progress, our community is the healthiest, safest and most prosperous place to raise children or crops or make widgets.

"Official business, Del?"

"Yes indeed, Marvin. Now that you're a local businessman, you'll be needing the services of the chamber to put your love counseling and fly tying service on the map. The *world* (he waved his arms) is waiting to hear about the (he looked out the front window at the sign) ... the *Fly Tying Love Center.*"

"Does it cost money to join?"

"Fifty bucks a year, Marvin. That's for a whole *year!*"

"And what do I get for that?"

"We list you on our chamber business list, and of course there's the monthly lunch meeting at the Mule Barn."

"Oh, you pay for lunch at the Mule Barn?"

"Uh ... no..."

"I eat there every day now, Del, and the guys tell me how to run my business and live my life, for free."

On the way back out to his car, Del thought how some businesses just weren't very progressive minded. Not at all.

Herb is a retired businessman, which tends to make the rest of us think he is practical. That wouldn't be entirely accurate, however, as Herb has the silent soul of a romantic. How else can anyone explain his passion for archery?

Most nice days he can be found out in his backyard, terrorizing a stack of hay bales with a target pinned to it. Many shooters do this, of course, but Herb is different. In this age of compound bows which resemble portable gym equipment, sights that glow in the dark, releases that resemble handguns, and arrows made of space-age materials, Herb is a throwback to the old days.

He shoots a wooden recurve bow and uses wooden arrows. His fingers and bow arm are protected by leather rather than plastic, and he trusts his own eye and form to place the arrow in the paper plate affixed to the hay bales.

Dud was watching him one afternoon.

"You shoot very well, Herb."

"Thanks."

"Wouldn't you get more speed from a compound bow and some graphite arrows?"

"Sure."

"Well ...?"

Herb smiled at him. "Dud, if I judged the fun of shooting by how fast I could get something to the target, I'd go in the house and get my deer rifle. It'll shoot circles around any bow ever made."

Herb hesitated a minute. "You see, Dud, if I hit the target, I want it to be mostly because I did it right and not some ammunition factory somewhere. I'm selfish. I want the credit ... and I'm willing to accept the blame if I miss."

It was a bright morning, and we had finished off the coffee and conversation at the Mule Barn truck stop, and we couldn't think of anything much to do because we were still full from breakfast and it was too early for lunch, and the political problems and Hollywood gossip tanks had been thoroughly topped off. So we went over to Doc's house to look at his mare in the back yard. She had, he said, a quarter crack in a front hoof.

So there we were, in a half circle around the little mare, staring at that slight crack as though focusing would bring a welded solution to the problem, but we all knew we just needed to drink Doc's coffee and change the scene.

"I see you have a block of salt," Bert said.

Doc nodded. Bert said, "Speaking of salt ..."

We really hadn't been, but smooth transitions aren't always easy.

".... puts me in mind of the time I stopped in that little store," Bert said. "Few years back now, I guess. Well, it was about the last time Milly had pups, because I think I'd left her home to have them. Of course, she waited until I got home ...."

Doc and Steve stared at him encouragingly. "And?"

"Oh ... well, there's this little store up north ... out in the middle of about flat nothing ... and it was hot and I was thinking of a nice cold cocola right about then, so I stopped."

Bert looked around. "Dang store was about full of salt."

"Salt?"

"Everywhere. This guy had ice cream salt. Bags of it. Salt blocks for horses, sheep, cows, rabbits and even danged guinea pigs. He had regular salt. He had huge bags of bulk salt for putting on the ice. He even had salt to make your water soft.

"So I went to pay for my drink and I says to the guy, 'You must sell a lot of salt.' And he says to me, 'No, but that salesman who calls on me sure does.'"

"Technology," said Bert the other day, "will save us all. Nothing like it. Just about the time you think you've seen it all, they come up with new flimdiddles that make life easier and faster for us all."

Doc looked up from his coffee. "I take it you have something specific in mind this fine day?"

"Hundreds of things," Bert says. "You know I read that science magazine. You can't believe what they're working on. Someday we'll be able to just stay home and watch television and earn a living. But the one that brought it to mind was our new dishwasher. Maizie and I found one the other day that just simplifies the whole process. They installed it yesterday and it works like a champ."

"Dishwashers? I don't like 'em at all," Dud said. "Heck, you have to wash the dishes before you put them in the machine, anyway. So I mean, why bother? You end up doing more work than if you didn't have one in the first place."

"Ah!" said Bert. "Just what I mean. Our last dishwasher was like that, but this one does that all in one step. You don't even need to rinse 'em off. Just stick 'em in there and turn the thing on. Kinda pricey, but worth it."

"Our dishwasher has done that for years now," Doc said. "Nothing new there. You don't need to rinse 'em first, and they come out sparkling clean every time."

"No kidding, Doc? What's the name of it?"

"Why, it's the Doc-O-Matic," he said, grinning. "It's worked well every day now since 1952. All you need is a sink."

We heard about the lemonade stand later, of course, as it was several blocks from where the rest of us lived, but it was only a couple of houses from Herb Collins. He had to go there. He couldn't resist.

The stand was set up by Heather and Tim Naismith, a sister/brother team whose ages added together wouldn't hit 18. Herb watched them set it up on that hot afternoon and finally couldn't stand it. He had to have some fun.

107

The lemonade was fifty cents, a bargain in anyone's book, as canned soda pop is running about a buck these days. And anyone can see that a lemonade stand set up by two youngsters is something to be encouraged. The free enterprise system at its very best. Ingenuity. American spirit. Besides, those Naismith kids are kinda cute, having worked so hard to get the lemonade made and the card table set up out under the tree in front.

Herb explained later that what he was really setting out to do, besides giving the kids some business, was to teach them a few harmless lessons in how to succeed in retail. Years ago, before he got into the trucking business, Herb ran a pawn shop in the city. He was known to be a sharp trader, and he delighted in telling us how little he paid for things and how much he sold them for.

"Hi kids," he told them. "Pretty good lemonade?"

"The best, Mr. Collins," Heather said.

"So ... fifty cents a glass? Well, all right, I'll have a glass."

He put down fifty cents and they filled a tall paper cup nearly to the brim for him. It was good lemonade.

"So how much for four glasses of lemonade?"

Tim did some silent figuring. "Two dollars, sir."

"Well, that's the retail price, of course," Herb said, "but now we're buying in bulk. What you do when someone wants to buy in bulk is you adjust the price. I think I should be able to buy four glasses of lemonade at, say, forty cents a glass. What do you think?"

The kids whispered in each other's ears.

"Mr. Collins," said Heather, "if you buy four glasses for forty cents each, how much would you expect to pay for a dozen glasses?"

Heartened by their interest in business, Herb said, "Oh, probably about thirty cents a glass, I guess. You have to make allowances for volume, you see."

"Good," said Heather. "We'll sell you a dozen glasses of lemonade, then, because we want to sell a lot of it, and we'll only charge you $3.60 for them."

Herb pulled out the money.

"But you'll have to drink them all here," Heather said. "We don't have a license for carry-out."

The evening was one of those that come back to you time after time, year after long year. It comes back and whispers of how good life can be when you're well fed, enjoying life, and a good friend shares the front porch with you on a summer's evening.

It was that way with Doc and Steve the other night. Doc thought he might have to do a scientific paper on the soporific effects of ice tea, fried chicken, and corn on the cob. As long as it didn't take any effort.

So when this huge meal had been bull-snaked down, the two grinning friends came out to the porch to watch the sun go down behind the trees along Lewis Creek. The air had that orange and russet glow, and the breeze, that little one that caresses the neck, came slowly down from the hills and made their shirt collars wiggle ever so slightly.

It was like taking a dry bath in paradise.

Doc sidled up to one of the porch posts and gently tested it to see if it could hold the extra weight he was carrying with that meal. It stood fine, so he leaned against it seriously and looked out on the evening's warmth.

Steve, who was enjoying having a fine meal that someone else cooked for a change, leaned against the post on the other side of the steps.

And then they just stood quietly, watching the day make beautiful skies as it ended.

The shadow on the ground foretold the presence of the circling bird. Doc and Steve paid no attention at first. Then a few minutes later, it was joined by two more circling birds over Doc's house.

"Buzzards," Steve mumbled.

"Yep," said Doc.

They circled some more.

"I think one of us should move a little …" said Doc.

"Move?"

"Well … to let them know … you know."

Steve sighed, then glanced over at Doc. "Flip you for it."

Only Dewey could do it. Our local disaster zone, Dewey, is one of the kindest hearted guys you ever met, but … well, things *happen* when Dewey's around.

He's finally settled into being what he calls an "entre-manure," hauling truckloads of cow manure from the feedlot and dairy into town and selling it for garden fertilizer. So recently we headed in to the Mule Barn truck stop for the morning coffee and philosophy encounter only to find our resident cowboy, Steve, moaning and holding his head in his hands.

"What's wrong?"

"Dewey," he moaned. It kinda came out *Dooo-eee* with a sad little droop there at the end. Sometimes there's a complete novel in the pronunciation of a name.

Turns out Bob Milford out at the Diamond W put out the word locally that he could use some help with the gather and branding. Steve and Dud both went to help, but so did Dewey. Bob didn't know what to do with Dewey, but finally put him on a gentle horse. After all, it's been two years since Dewey helped Bob with the branding and managed to vaccinate Dud for blackleg.

"We were doing all right and working along this ridge," says Steve, "when here comes ol' Dewey just a foggin' it and he tells us we have to help him because he has a cow up a tree."

Oh yeah. This is gonna be good.

"Seems Dewey choused this old black baldy cow right off this big rock outcropping and she landed in the forks of a tree below. He was almost hysterical. So we looked at this and Bob told Dud to go back to the truck and get the chainsaw.

"And you should've heard Dewey begging us not to cut up the cow because it was all his fault." Steve grinned and shook his head. "We just let him go on like that until we cut the tree down."

I took my homemade pirogue out on Miller Pond the other day. The yellow one with black trim. I call it *"Bayou Banana,"* of course. It was a nice kind of day, sunny and warm, no wind. I paddled around for about an hour, I guess. Good exercise, right? A relaxing paddle, right?

Not in this flat-bottomed Cajun canoe, and not on Miller Pond.

Because when I first launched the pirogue, it became the *Golden Hind*, sailing into San Francisco Bay for the first time, allowing me to claim California for the British. Then, as I neared the point, out came the Iroquois in their war canoes, and I had to paddle like crazy and duck the arrows as I tried to keep them from taking my beaver pelts and my life.

But I made it.

Then, in the middle of a calm, warm afternoon, Miller Pond became the stormy Atlantic as my square-rigged ship tossed in the grip of the hurricane. I stayed glued to the helm and kept her bow facing the blast. We rode each mountainous wave to the top and then hurtled down the other side into a trough filled with dread and death. And just when the men had given up, my skillful paddling sent us safely climbing yet another monstrous sea into the sunlight of victory and life.

When the storm subsided, I spied an enemy warship, laden to the gunwales with high explosives. So heavily laden was it, actually, that all you could see was its eyes and nose and the slight rudderly switch of his tail as it camouflaged itself as a muskrat.

But there in my submarine, the crew was alert to these ruses. Swiftly and silently I turned the submarine until its forward torpedo tubes faced the enemy warship. As I watched through the periscope for any sign that their deck crew had spotted us, I gave the orders.

"Fire one! Fire two!"

"Torpedoes running hot, straight and normal, sir," said my second-in-command, who resembles a coonhound in civilian life.

Blam! Blam! Dead-center hits on the warship, which strangely kept going until it rounded a point in the ocean, preferring to sink privately, out of sight of its conquerors.

Then the armada was sighted, closing in on the north of Ireland. It looked a lot like Herb Collins in his new dory. As the armada swung around to face our guns, I took note of the dory's clean lines, the upswept bow and stern. It reminded me a lot of a World War II battleship.

I gotta get me one of those.

Doc was out back of his place the other day, pruning his grapevines with the kind of precision only a semi-retired practicing surgeon can do. Steve was standing nearby, sipping a soda and watching Doc work.

There was a rasping sound then, dopplering over Doc's yard from east to west. Doc, without looking up, said, "Morning Wheezer."

"Didn't catch that, Doc."

"That's ol' Wheezer," Doc said, waving his hand up toward the heavens. "Didn't you hear him? Mourning dove. Lives here and in the yards on either side. Something's wrong with his voice."

"Ah," said Steve, the cowboy philosopher. He nodded and tried to

111

look wise, but only managed a tilt-headed owl look. But at least he does it well.

Doc sat back and smiled up at Steve. "Ol' Wheeze there, he's been around for three years I know of. When he flies over, I always say hello to him. Must be getting old, talking to doves, huh?"

"What's wrong with his voice?" Steve asked.

"I'm no vet," said Doc, "but if you'll go catch him, we can check him out."

They both laughed.

"The only reason I know he's a he is because I saw him courting this cute little lady dove this spring. She thought his raspy ol' voice was charming and wonderful," Doc said.

"He goes over on Vivian's roof sometimes, and then back over to Rob's place, but mainly he lives on my roof and in the tree branches."

Steve sent his face into philosophizing mode. Anyone could see that right off.

"Whatcha thinkin', Steve?"

"Just occurred to me, Doc," he said. "You've learned a lot about this bird, and have made him your friend, in a way. And you've been able to follow his actions and family life and everything. And none of that would've been possible if ol' Wheezer didn't have a speech impediment. Without that, he'd be just another bird. Looks like one time when a handicap made life a bit more interesting."

"It happens that way sometimes," Doc agreed.

It was a silent thing there at first. It was the calm mornings that did it. Each of us became quieter when having breakfast at the Mule Barn truck stop. We'd look at each other and smile and wish each other well without having to say anything. It was a summer thing.

Each of us had our own jobs, which ranged from Dewey's transferring manure from the dairy to people's yards, through Bert's obsession with weeding his yard, to Doc's trying to keep us healthy. Herb Collins came in that morning. Herb is a businessman, not too excited about sports, but keen on being one of the guys. He also claims to be borderline psychic. We always thought he was a little strange on that account.

Until that summer morning.

"Politics going along fine, are they?" Herb asked the quiet philosophy counter.

Guys nodded and murmured.

"Somebody sick?"

Heads shook, still with the faraway look in the eyes.

"It's the Lunker, isn't it?" Herb asked.

All heads perked up, and we looked at each other with that sudden recognition. Yes, it was the Lunker, that giant trout down in his pool in Lewis Creek.

Doc was the first to recognize that Herb was right. "What do you think, guys … tomorrow morning?"

"I'll bring coffee," said Dud.

"I'm going to catch him," Dewey said.

"No worms, Dewey. Barbless flies only."

Dewey nodded.

"I'm going to try a new fly," Dud said. "Tied some up after I saw them in the magazine. Supposed to be deadly on trout."

"I'm glad you're going, Dud," Doc said. "I'll need a witness when I pull him in."

The Lunker rose close to a couple of the flies the next day, and some smaller trout fell for them and were quickly released. The Lunker is still under that big pile of rocks on the bottom of Lewis Creek.

And that's not an altogether bad thing. Dreams are good.

We'd never seen Doc quite as much in his element as he was Saturday. Those of us who love this aging healer were as proud of his accomplishment as he was. It's strange how someone so instrumental in our lives can take pride in something that is of seemingly little importance, and that's how it was with Doc.

He's been a doctor here for so many years that legend status caught up with him and passed him ages ago.

But a few years ago, Doc got the idea of becoming a viticulturalist – a wine maker. He sent off for some high-class grapevines and got them growing out behind the corral at his place. In a few years, they were making grapes. Then Doc – having read everything on grapes including Bacchus's own diary – made some wine, bottled it, and set it aside to age. To age, that is, until Saturday's unveiling.

113

He had his wife, Mrs. Doc, print up some labels on the computer, and the result was three bottles of wine. And so, to the accompaniment of cheese and crackers, he threw a wine tasting. Naturally, since we were his fellow co-conspirators at the Mule Barn truck stop's world-dilemma think tank, we were invited.

It was great. Mrs. Doc had candles lighted and some soft music going on the stereo, and everyone got a sip and some munchies. Doc was congratulated, and he was living it up.

Steve, the resident cowboy of our little group, took Doc to one side with a question.

"How soon can you be in production, Doc?"

Doc lit up. "You think I should?"

"Sure. In fact, do you have any more of this wine here, you know, that I could buy from you?"

"Sorry, Steve," Doc said, "but this is all of it. You really like it, huh?"

"Well, no," Steve said, "but I've got this utility sink with a blocked drain pipe…"

Dud and I had just about finished solving the problems on page one and were about to start solving sports dilemmas when Bert mumbled something. Now Bert, usually loquacious, was in one of his rare, but deadly, silent coffee mornings. Normally he'd fill the Mule Barn truck stop with his pronouncements on life, love, literature and the price of cauliflower, but not today.

I took a sip and turned to Bert. "You say something, Bert?"

"Seeds and froth," he mumbled.

"Seeds and froth?"

"It's not like it was my fault, you know. What did I do? Hey, sometimes seeds and froth just happen to people, and there's no need to jump all over me about it."

Dud and I nodded as if we understood. We assumed more would be coming. It was.

"I mean, is it a crime to own a mule? No. So I own a mule. So seeds and froth come along and the mule owner gets it? Where's the justice in that? Ol' Jack was hungry. Is that a crime now? And is it my fault? I don't think so."

"How is ol' Jack, anyway?" We all knew and loved the stove-up old retired mule that Bert took so much pride in.

"He's in the doghouse big time with Maizie," Bert said. "Why shouldn't she shoulder some responsibility for the seeds and froth? I mean, you could actually give her some of the blame for this mess, you know. She's the one left the car window down."

"Do I have to hurt you, Bert?"

"Huh? Oh, well, see, here's what happened. Maizie did the shopping and drove in the yard, and you know how ol' Jack likes to be loose and wander around the yard, right? So she took some groceries in the house, but not all of them, and Jack found the passenger window open and when she came back...."

He put his head in his hands.

"How was I supposed to know mules liked watermelon? You guys ever feed watermelon to a mule? Me neither. *Who knew?* By the time Maizie got back for her next load, ol' Jack had eaten about two thirds of that watermelon on the seat. Man, there were seeds and froth all over the seat, the floor, the door and the mule. And I swear ... I *swear* to you ... he started grinning when he saw her coming back out of the house."

"And I guess you had to clean it up."

He nodded. "Dang mule has the table manners of a two-year-old. When you mix seeds and froth with mule slobber? Well ... don't do it."

According to the calendar, when we get to September each year, the earth has tilted on its axis and the days are getting shorter, and we aren't barbecuing as much as we did a month ago.

But no one told September that summer was over. So we usually get one farewell blast of heat straight from the hinges of perdition and we look at each other and say, "I thought it was supposed to be September." But we laugh, too, because we do this every September.

I think, if the truth be known, we don't splash in the swimming hole in Lewis Creek as much in September simply because it's September, and we don't think we should. And the barbecue tongs are polished up and put away until Memorial Day because it's supposed to be September.

But during the intense heat of September, we are finding ourselves looking forward to the fall, to the hunt, to the cold weather, to ... yes ... shoveling snow. Our thoughts are more with Halloween than with picnics. We want to buy a new shirt for fall, even knowing that if we tried it on now, we'd have heat stroke and die.

We're never really content, are we? All during the spring winds and the rain we looked forward to summer, and tied fishing flies daily as homage to the heat of the sun to come. We checked the boat long before the water was warm enough to fish in. We sharpened the blades on the lawn mower when the grass was still brown and looking dead.

Hurry, next season. We've had this one, and now we're ready for it to be over. Hurry, autumn. Bring us the orange and black and the coral and gold of the trees. Make us ready for that first brisk day that tells us we are still here for another turning of the seasons.

We're ready for fall.

"It's just not the same," said Steve. "I don't care how you want to call it, it just isn't the same thing any more."

"But it does make sense," said Doc. "I personally think catch-and-release fishing is a good thing. Hey, how many fish can a guy eat, anyway? This way, we have all the fun of catching them, and then we turn them loose and catch 'em again later, if they're stupid enough to fall for the same bait."

We sucked down some more coffee and got refilled. Doc put his hand over his cup when Loretta came by. He's trying to cut back on the caffeine. He's not a kid any more, of course.

"Catch-and-release fishing," said Dud, in his most pontifical voice, "is here to stay. It is the future. It guarantees us that we will always have a good supply of fish. I don't mind crimping the barbs on my hooks at all."

He made an arm gesture not unlike those made by Hitler when stirring up the masses.

"From this day forth," Dud said, "the world will see that catch-and-release will bring forth hundreds of fish, thousands of fish, untold *millions* upon *millions* of fish where before there was simply (his voice quieted right here) a few. A vagrant *few*. A piddly selection of piscatorial beasts gracing our streams and ponds."

Dud was in rare form for just three cups of coffee here at the Mule Barn.

"Yea, verily," he said, waving his spoon, "just take Lewis Creek, that last bastion of the monster of the deep ... The Lunker. With catch-and-release, he can get married and have pups and replenish his part of the earth. We'll be overrun with lunkers."

"But it's still not the same," said Steve, in his cowboy manner. "I went out and hooked a big one and took its picture and turned it loose, but it wasn't the same as being able to weigh it and measure it."

"How big was it?" asked Doc.

"Hard to say, Doc," Steve said, "but the picture weighed six and a half pounds."

Autumn

There's a reason most county and state fairs are held in the fall: this is when we are at our best. We've canned the fruit and raised the calves and our tan was never tanner. In the woods, the deer's antlers are at their shiniest and sharpest and the trees are blessed with red and gold. We are as polished as we're going to get, and it's a time to make more memories and laugh with our families.
Autumn is what we get for being good all year.

Sweet transition from the heat, from the work, from the hard, rough edges of life. On we go now to autumn, to black, lacy leaves and twigs standing out against an orange sky. The mornings now have that coolness, that chill that tells us we once again have made it through the heat and toil and can sit back now and then and reflect on things.

We can think now of family, of children growing and learning. We can think of loved ones growing old and feeble, but even more beloved as we realize what treasures they are to us.

We can think back on childhood memories of lazy mornings in church, when the droning kept us in constant danger of sleep, of the smell of coffee, of the taste of purloined doughnuts and the sweet frosting on them.

We can think back to the fires of spring, when we found that love is not only terrible, but terribly exciting, too. We can reflect on moments so sacred they live only within our souls and are never expressed, because no one is good enough to put the right words to them.

We look at red barns and horses starting to shag up for winter. We think of the woods, and the deer, and the creeks running pure clear and cold with fish and quiet. The evenings now, the quiet fall evenings when we see the first star come out right over the town where it has always been and we once again ask ourselves if it has always been this way and do we make a difference, or is this simply a chance for our souls to slide through a beautiful time known as life.

We settle down now to an earlier bed time, to a later getting up time, to savoring the heat of the morning coffee as well as the smell and the taste. We look around, now that the fever of summer work has abated, and we notice people and pets and neighbors that are precious to us, and we give a little smile and nod, which means, "I love you, too."

It was just one of those crazy mix-ups, you know. Like when one thing goes wrong it triggers another thing that goes wrong and that sets off a multiplicity of crash-and-burns that are remembered long after people are dead and nations fall to Visigoths and such.

That's what happened with our buddy, Dud. You see, he was *there* at a time when something was needed, and he stepped forward and assumed the role.

It was the high school band, of course. We love them. There aren't that many of them, but they're great kids and try hard, and Mr. Garcia has really whipped them into something that can carry a tune. Every honk and wheeze was special to us. So when the planets lined up the wrong direction and Sagittarius was in the outhouse or something, Dud was there.

It began when Mr. Garcia got called away on a family emergency. His dad, I think. So he wouldn't be at the pep rally before the football game. Another teacher was planning to step in and lead the band through the cheers, but the entire horn section, all four of them, came down sick.

So it was decided that the band wouldn't play at the pep rally this time, and the cheerleaders would just cheer *a capella*, as it were.

We were surprised when Dud walked into the auditorium carrying his accordion and waving to the crowd. He sat down out front and began to play waltzes and a couple of polkas. The cheerleaders didn't know what to do to "The Tennessee Waltz," so they just sat down and waited for Dud to run out of tunes. It didn't take long.

We sorta clapped at the end there, mostly from relief.

Later, over coffee, Dud was still on a high.

"Did you guys like the music? I knew I could help."

"Well," said Doc, "maybe if you could find some Sousa marches for the accordion."

"That would help, eh?"

"Well, that, and having Mr. Garcia back."

Genius is occasionally driven by desperation, and that's what happened to Annette down at the Soup 'R Market.

The phone lines were fuzzy that day, she thinks, because of an electrical storm. That's the only reason she can think of that she was stuck with 800 pounds of squash. She thought she was ordering 80 pounds, you see, but there was static … oh well.…

So the banner went up across the front of the market. It was so thick you had to duck under it to get in the store. "Giant Squash Recipe Contest," it read.

This was fascinating, because science and mothers have been trying for centuries to make squash edible to normal human beings. Some thought it wasn't possible, but those folks probably think we didn't land on the moon, either. In most of us there is this innate belief that someone will someday make squash into an edible vegetable.

Of course, we've been wrong before.

To enter Annette's giant squash recipe contest, you had to first register at the store, and then pick out the kind of squash you want to transform into food. Then you bring the completed dish in on Saturday at 11 a.m., along with the recipe all written out. The entries would be tasted by blindfolded locals whose wives had volunteered them for the task.

By Tuesday the squash began being sold so fast that Annette's kid had to continually bring more from the back of the store to refill the bins.

Zuccini was a favorite, closely followed by crookneck.

On Saturday, quite a crowd had gathered, because it turned out that many of the local cooks thought their family recipe could turn gourds into a meal. The blindfolded judges were unanimous in picking Carla Martinez's squash dish, which had enough chile in it to disguise brunch at Lucretia Borgia's. After the applause, Carla proudly drove home with her prize: one hundred pounds of squash.

We sure have fun around here.

We all read about Pastor Jeff's latest tribulation in the local paper, the Valley Weekly Miracle. Maybe tribulation is too strong a word, because, after all, when someone leaves your church a huge legacy, isn't it time for rejoicing? Shouldn't we all be walking around the walls of Jericho tootling on ram's horns and beating the drums in jubilation?

It seems one of Pastor Jeff's former church members - a kinda strange former church member - went off to the city some years ago and became a fairly well-known painter of pictures. When this eccentric artist went to that great studio in the sky recently, leaving no family, his will left everything to Pastor Jeff's congregation. There was a little money, which was welcomed, naturally, but the main item was paintings. More than a thousand of them. They are now the property of Pastor Jeff's church. They have filled the basement with them and they're threatening to crowd the pie-cooling counter in the ladies' kitchen area, which just can't happen.

They must be sold, of course, but there is one catch: none of them are named, and everyone knows a painting must have a name or else it's not a *real* work of art. These paintings are from the school of abstract expressionism, which means there's a lot of bright paint on them, and if you can look at one and figure out what it's supposed to be, the artist failed.

A painting-naming committee was formed, naturally, and the last we heard, had about a dozen paintings named, based loosely on what some wild curve or blob on the canvas brought to someone's mind.

Of course, down at the Mule Barn truck stop's philosophy counter and world dilemma think tank, we came up with a solution in about three cups' time.

The trick, we decided, is to blend nonsensical words together, because anyone who would buy one of these paintings has an obvious contempt for reality in the first place. So we came up with a formula. Make a list and name a painting an *amalgamation/dynamism/cataclysm/rudiment/ despotism/heraldry/approximation*

of

sin/pulchritude/embellishment/innocence/hitchiking/world order/fishing season/spaghetti feeds/lassitude/ennui/cyclamates.

You simply pick one from one column, one from the other column, slap 'em together and there you go. With seven in the first column and 11 in the second column, the naming committee can instantly name at least 77 paintings. And this was just during three cups of Mavis's best. A hard-working church committee could name a thousand paintings during one of Pastor Jeff's sermons and be back in business in time for the benediction.

We drove up the mountain as far as Jasper Blankenship's cabin, then walked in the remaining quarter mile to Steve's newly built cabin. We all knew how important this mountain hideaway was to the semi-aging cowboy, and were prepared to ooh and aah in unison. A cabin, for a man who never had a home that he owned, is a big deal.

He'd been working on building the place for months now, ever since he gave up trying to figure out how to put a cabin on a lot that was skinnier than the cabin. He finally found an acre right where he wanted it. Finally, over coffee down at the Mule Barn, he said he was ready for visitors as long as we didn't need anything more complicated than a cup of coffee and a chair.

We made a morning expedition of it. But when we came in sight of the cabin hiding in the dense shade of the pines, we weren't ready for what we found. Steve had built a turret on one corner. A turret. A little room 'way up *there*.

"Like my turret?" he said.

"Well," said Doc, "it sure looks … well made."

"You don't think it's pretty?"

"Sure we do!" said Herb. "It's just …"

"Just what?"

"A … turret. You know. We weren't expecting one."

"You can go in it, but it only holds one at a time. Have to climb a ladder."

"Me first," said Dud, and went through the front door.

We all took our turns up in the turret. It had a chair next to an end table with magazines on it. There was a window on each wall. You could see half the world.

Doc finally climbed down the ladder and poured himself a coffee. "Got to tell you, Steve, I never had you figured for a turret man."

Steve smiled into his coffee, then looked up. "If you guys each built a cabin exactly the way you wanted it … no women or anything in the planning … you know … wouldn't you have a turret?"

We thought about that for minute, then … slowly, the supreme court of coffee drinkers began nodding collectively.

Then Dud said, "And mine would have a TV set …"

To look at Herb Collins, you wouldn't think he was like that. A nicer, kinder guy you never met. But for one evening each year … one little slice of time … he's downright diabolical.

Every small town has one, of course. There is always that one person who takes Halloween to its extremes of horror and fantasy. We have Herb.

Everyone knows about his penchant for decoration. Ever since he retired, his yard and house has celebrated every holiday from Christmas to Amelia Earhart's wedding anniversary with great festoonation and an increase in the electrical bill from all the lights.

But on Halloween, Herb goes plumb nuts. It's a good thing heart trouble is rare for the age group who go trick or treating, because Herb's yard is a veritable booby trap of pouncing ghosts, swooping bats that swing out of the trees, loud sound effects as witches pop straight out of the lawn in front of children and cackle, and porch-side demons that shriek and leap just as the kid reaches what he considers the safety of Herb's front porch.

It's a running of the gauntlet that only the bravest of the brave attempt. Herb says he hasn't had a four-year-old make it to the front door yet. But for the older kids, this is an annual challenge, and one by one they leave the safety of the sidewalk to do a broken-field run, often with screaming, until they hit the safety of the doorbell. Once that doorbell rings, they know, it's all over but the candy.

Ah, the candy! As if to make up for all the screaming and terror, Herb gives out dollar candy bars. Some kids have been known to carry them around for several days to show off before eating them.

"It gives the little guys something to shoot for," Herb says, laughing. "And the big guys get a different dose of demons every year so they aren't sure what to expect."

And Herb?

"I just have a lot of fun."

This is the polished time, the pinnacle of life. This is fall, when everything puts on its best for the world to see, and that makes it special.

The sultry heat of summer has passed, and in its place we have cool mornings when the tiny snap of winter's promise briefly touches our skin. There is a magic quality of light and feel in the air, and those of us who enjoy the outdoors know it's time to go to camp. In our genes, we know it's time to go to camp. It's time to be in the woods with rod and bow and gun and rediscover ourselves.

In town, it's time for the kids to be back in school, giving their mothers time to think about themselves for a while. Time to consider if taking a class wouldn't be a fun idea, or planning a small business that wouldn't interfere too much with the family.

The antlers of the deer have now been polished to a bone white at the tips and a rugged brown elsewhere. They are prime, as is their owner. It is fall. It is the polished time. The trees, as the sap shuts down in the leaves, share their gold and reds with us and make commonplace scenes only a few weeks ago into magical tapestries of nature.

It is the time of finding a mate, of fighting for territory, of defining our lives. It is fall. And we know we must polish ourselves a little bit right now in order to fit in. We have to assess ourselves and ask what we can do to make our lives a little shinier, our hopes a little stronger, our promises to others more defined, more definite.

It is a looking around time. A savoring time. It is the time to let the fresh cool air fill our lungs and let us remember other falls, other campfires, other friends. Younger friends, as we were younger. And as the golden leaves fall in the late autumn breezes, it will be time once again to cherish our mates and seek refuge from the winter wind.

Janice Thomas hasn't spent 23 years of her life teaching art appreciation and history for nothing. As with all teaching, she learned more than the students, naturally, and has taken pride in seeing several of them go on to dabble fairly successfully in the world of art.

That's why, two years ago, she took up the brush herself and got with the program. The early results were less than overwhelming. Her painting of Joe's barn, I recall, made the old structure lean even more than in real life. She said this painting was "representational," or "realistic." No one seemed to want to buy that painting, so she gave it to Joe. We didn't see it hanging in Joe's house later, either.

So Janice then began painting vases with flowers in them. Made them look kinda out of focus and gentle, but you couldn't really tell what kind of flowers they were. She entered it in a local art show as being "impressionistic," but it didn't make much of an impression on the judges.

A true artist never gives up, however. Janice's next work took her weeks and weeks. She painted a castle on the hill, we think. But it was a castle that kinda, well, *melted*. Called it "Existential Overlook." She said this kind of painting was "modernistic."

The judges didn't like that one, either, and didn't tell her why.

Next thing we know, she's loaded her 12 gauge with tiny capsules of paint, backed off about 20 yards from a sheet of plywood, and blew it into glorious color. She sawed around the colored part and put a nice frame on it.

She got an honorable mention down in the city at the art show,
too. When the judges asked what school of painting this was, she said,

"Ballistic."

⮞⮜

There was Steve, our resident cowboy, sitting at the round table in the Mule Barn truck stop, doodling on paper. Other members of the world dilemma think tank gravitated to Steve's table.

Steve appeared to be oblivious of the rest of us. "Downspout," he mumbled.

Doc nodded at Herb. "Downspout, Herb."

"I thought so, too," Herb said.

"Oh hi guys," said Steve.

"So Steve … downspout?"

"Hot tub," Steve said, as if that cleared everything up. "For the cabin. You know. I'm going to put in a hot tub."

"And you need a downspout for this?" Herb said.

"For the rain," Steve said.

We looked at him.

"No water," Steve said. "You know, at the cabin."

"Let's see if I have this right," Dud said. "You want to put a hot tub in at your cabin and you don't have water."

"Exactly."

"So you need a downspout…?"

"For when it rains," Steve said. "To fill the hot tub."

"Okay. So how will you get it hot?"

"Going to wrap copper tubing around the stovepipe in the cabin, you see, and then send it on out to the hot tub. The tub will be outside on the porch."

"You don't have a porch."

"But I will by the time I get the hot tub built," Steve explained. "I'll bet that copper tubing will heat that water right up and then I can have a good soak up there any time I want."

"Not quite," said Doc. "Not the way I figure it."

Steve looked at him. "Why not?"

"If the water comes down the downspout, around the stovepipe through the copper tubing and then outside to the hot tub, it looks to me like the only time you can soak in the tub is in a rainstorm."

Steve thought about that for a minute. Then sipped his cold coffee. Loretta heated it up.

⮞

"And Steve," said Doc, "you ever been on that mountain when the lightning's popping? If you're in that hot tub, with your moustache flopping around in the wind while you watch the surrounding countryside explode, well ..."

Steve wiped out what he was drawing with the pencil and started in on a fresh napkin.

He looked up after a few minutes. "Pool table," he said.

It's a good thing dreams are free.

"I need to know what you think, Sarah, because you're a business woman."

"Well ... OK, Delbert," she said. "What's up?"

"Fall colors," said Delbert McLain, our chamber of commerce here in the valley. He's our chamber of commerce because no one else wanted it.

Stopping her stocking of the shelves in the "Politics and more Humor" section of her "Read Me Now" bookstore, Sarah said, "The truth is, Delbert, I like fall colors."

"No, no ... not what I mean. I mean, can we convince people to come here and look at trees this time of year? It would do great things for the motels and our cafés ... to say nothing of the bookstore."

"Oh yes," she smiled, "that should start a run on the bookstore."

"We could print brochures. Fall colors. Maybe something enticing people to stay in a local motel and have Thanksgiving dinner at Chin's Chinese restaurant or the Mule Barn?"

"Thanksgiving is usually a time for families to get together, you know."

"I know it," he said, smacking his fist into his hand in frustration. "We need to change the initial concept of Thanksgiving. Like 'This year, celebrate *not* having relatives over. Come see us for colorful leaves and turkey down at the truck stop.'"

Sarah thought about it a minute.

"Do we really have to turn *every* holiday into a money maker for the town?"

He looked shocked. "It's ... it's *progress*, Sarah."

Sarah looked out at the clear sunlight making jacketed people's faces sparkle on the streets. Each one was a friend. Each one had problems and triumphs and also had within them blessings for the whole community.

"Delbert," she said, finally. "Maybe it would be best to let Thanksgiving alone and concentrate on another holiday where we don't have so much emotion tied up in it."

"Halloween?"

"How about Millard Fillmore's wedding anniversary?"

In our part of the country, fall means deer hunting. Many of us will dress up like a pile of leaves, go out into very cold weather, and sit still until we freeze to death.

Why? Because we want to have some venison this winter for the family. We'll figure out how much the venison costs us ... but only at gunpoint. Because this is not the most fiscally sane thing we do each year. Sanity would send us to buy some really tender beef to eat, but where's the glory in that? No, there are still a lot of us who would rather go out and find the meat and bring it home. And we spend a lot of money each year, and read lots of books and magazines, and talk endlessly about techniques. It doesn't appear to be a rational way to live, but when you apply science, history, anthropology and Darwinian theory, it still doesn't make any sense. But you sound more educated talking about it.

Doc's awfully good at that. When the subject came up the other day at the morning meeting of the world dilemma think tank (held daily at the Mule Barn truck stop since the Hoover administration) Doc said there was actually a very clear scientific reason for it.

"In cave days," he said, "only the best hunters lived to sire children. The others ate weeds and died a sorry death. So we come from a solid line of successful hunters. We've been running around clubbing things to death for about two million years that we know of, and we only started agriculture about 12,000 years ago. So if you divide this and carry the one ... well, another way to look at it is ... if man emerged from the trees a year ago, he was nothing but a hunter until 18 hours ago."

"Makes sense," said Dud, "think I'll buy some of that Autumn Fandango camo this year."

It was the cold outside that bound us together better inside the Mule Barn truck stop. The coffee warmed our innards and the laughter at the philosophy counter heated our souls to very comfortable.

It was Doc who noticed it first. He's trained to be observant, of course.

"Dudley, me lad," said Doc, "are you on a diet?"

Dud, whose body would fall into the "just right" category, shook his head.

"Not me, Doc. Why do you ask?"

"Every day, for years, you put sugar in your coffee. You didn't this morning."

Dud straightened himself up grandly and turned to his rapt audience.

"I discovered something about myself, Doc. Yes, in looking over my life, I've come to a conclusion.

"It all began right after Anita and I were married last year," Dud said. "One morning she came up and whispered to me that my life would be greatly enriched if I were to remove that dead tree in the back yard.

"Then she made me my favorite breakfast one morning, French toast with sourdough bread, and she sat in my lap and said if that sagging post on the porch were to be replaced, it just might cause extreme happiness to burst forth upon our stage."

"Is there a point to this?" Steve asked.

Dud sipped his coffee and grinned.

"So last month, she came up behind me and put her arms around my neck and started feminine-wiling me and asked if I'd get my pickup painted so she wouldn't be embarrassed when she rode with me."

"Dud," said Doc, "I can see your truck isn't painted, and I drove by the other day and your porch post still leans, and I thought I noticed that dead tree still out in your back yard."

"You're right, Doc. That was my big discovery and why I no longer put sugar in my coffee."

The others stared at Dud.

Dud just grinned. "I found out I'm sucrose intolerant."

In September, Jasper Blankenship comes down from his cabin on the mountain for several reasons. He has to gather supplies for the winter, which includes a whopping amount of chainsaw gas, of course. It gets cold up there.

There are groceries, too, and new doodads he's had time to peruse in the mail order catalogs over the summer months. But there's also his time with the kids. Jasper brings his fiddle down the mountain with him, buys some new strings for it if necessary, and then heads over to the school. Little kids are his specialty.

"Kindergarteners and first graders are really interested in music," he says. "They seem to have more of an appreciation for the finer things. When they turn into second graders, life seems to be more … well, they just kinda turn cynical on a guy."

His instrument is technically a violin, of course, but the way he plays it, and the kind of music he plays make it a fiddle. Forget the ballads of Bartok, the concertos of Tchaikovsky, the sweet sounds of Smetana. None of these are in Jasper's repertoire, nor are they ever likely to be. His music is that of the barn dances, the tall hills of our land, the sweet ramblings of Celtic music his ancestors brought with them from England, Ireland and Scotland. He learned his music strictly by ear, and learned it from sitting late at night outside dance halls, listening to the fiddles when he was too young to go in, and then taking his memories home and learning each tune on his fiddle.

So he plays for the little guys at school, and tells them stories. And he always waits until one of the children notices that the last joint on one of his fingers on the left hand is missing, the result of a farming accident in his youth. Of course, that's not what he tells the kids.

"When I was a boy," he says, holding up the partial digit in question, "we didn't have enough money for real violin strings. I had to use barbed wire."

George down at the paint store managed to pull off something no one ever thought possible; he found, wooed and wed a woman without everyone in town knowing about it.

In a community where everyone knows how many times a day each person brushes his teeth, and how many teeth each one of us has, this was something of a miracle.

George isn't a young man, and he'd been widowed for more than 10 years. His children were grown and married, except for Elwood, his son who lives just out of town on a little place out there. The amazing thing was, we discovered, Elwood didn't know about this, either.

One day George showed up at church with a very friendly lady on his arm and asked Pastor Jeff if he could speak for a second. Jeff said sure, and George stood and introduced Judy, his new bride, to the congregation.

Immediately, the underground telegraph went to work. The Curl Up 'N Dye beauty parlor investigative team sprang into action. Who is Judy? Where's she from? Who are her people?

Your people are very important here, of course, as we are firm believers that the acorn doesn't fall far from the tree.

Elwood was waylaid one morning as he foolishly walked past the beauty parlor. He was snatched in as though hooked to a vacuum cleaner. All he knew, he told them, was that Judy seemed really nice, and that she was from the city, and that his dad and Judy had written each other for a long time.

The term "mail order bride" was bandied about by one or two members of the curler crew, but of course it wasn't true and didn't take. He courted her fair and square by postage stamp until they both got computers and made faster connections.

George told us. We cornered him for coffee one morning and asked about the courting procedures and all that. He told us he "had" to get married.

Our jaws dropped, and then he laughed and said he "had to get married because I couldn't afford the phone bill any more."

A guy that good at keeping a secret in this valley would make a great spy.

The first one to come in was the flicker. Later, when the others showed up, I called him Flicker #1. He landed on a branch near me and never even looked my way. He scratched his face with a claw and looked around, then flew up to a nearby aspen tree.

I was invisible, you see. I had taken my alfalfa pills each day before the hunt, to destroy human odor, and then I dressed like a pile of leaves … we hunters call it camo … to finish the job.

Flickers #2 and #3 landed on dead aspen logs, which lay as starkly bleached bones of the forest, and then the birds playfully attacked each other. Something at my feet drew my attention. About six feet from my boots, a mouse came out of a hole in a rotten stump and looked around. He stared at the quarreling woodpeckers, then looked to the sky for hawks or owls, or maybe just to check the weather. I was a Brobdingnabian giant many hundreds of times his size and weight, but he didn't see me or even look my way. He began whisking then. He'd whisk to the right and look for stuff. Then he'd whisk to the left, and this time he found a tiny seed and decided soup was on. To my amazement, he sat on his haunches and ate this seed less than a foot from my left boot. Two seeds later, he ducked back down his hole to check on the kids, while I sat saturated in the golden anticipation of the hunt. I swiveled my neck again to see if any suicidal deer had stopped by my hidden ground blind.

Nope.

Back at the Mule Barn for lunch, Doc asked if I'd seen any deer.

"Not this morning," I said, grinning to myself. "Nice weather, though."

Hey, there's more to bowhunting than just shooting arrows.

Dud brought the accordion in the other day. Right there in the Mule Barn truck stop, in the middle of hot cakes and coffee and grits.

We groaned as he opened the case and lifted the shiny Stomach Steinway and pulled the straps over his shoulders. We hadn't heard Dud play since the band director got sick before a pep rally last fall and Dud filled in for the band. Of course, waltzes weren't exactly what the kids were needing to get their blood up before a football game. We lost.

"You're not going to play that, are you?" asked Doc, trying to pry his eyes open.

Dud nodded and grinned, popping open the bellows release snaps top and bottom.

"Before coffee?" wailed Steve.

"It's a known scientific fact," said Herb, "that music can help you digest your food, and put you in a better mood to start your day."

Steve pelted Herb with cracker packets. Herb hadn't heard Dud try to fire up the offensive line with the Altenhauer Waltz, after all. We had.

As we were looking to see if the exits were blocked, Dud began to play. And we stopped and smiled and raised our cups to Dud. The waitresses smiled. The cook came out of the kitchen.

Hey ... he got *good!*

Dud started with a couple of sweet, flowing waltzes, and then swung   133 into some light polkas. So there we were, at seven in the morning, dancing between tables with Mavis and Loretta and keeping them from their coffee pouring, and we didn't care, and they didn't care, and Dud kept playing and....

... well, I mean the Mule Barn's owner had a point, after all. It *was* the breakfast rush, after all, and we *were* keeping the waitresses from waiting. And the French toast doesn't cook itself when Bernie the cook is dancing through the lobby with Mrs. Lawson from down the street.

So Dud put the squeezebox back into its case and we turned back to solving the world's problems. But we were smiling more than we usually do at that time of the morning. By golly, ol' Dud really has been practicing. We're proud of him.

Doc summed it up best. "Dud ... if you were to play for a pep rally now, I believe we'd win."

Mickey Baker has owned The Strand – our local movie theater – since the new releases starred Virginia Mayo. The Strand, naturally, is an icon here. More than a few of our long-lasting marriages in the area began with a first date there. Most of us have consumed more than our share of Raisinettes and Jujubes while watching Duke Wayne whip the bad guys. We know every inch of The Strand. We know where the rips are in the used-to-be blood-red carpet, which seats don't fold all the way down, which seats are most secluded in case it's a smooching date. It was ol' Dud, back when he was about four feet tall, who discovered how to combine chewing gum and the lock on the back door to provide five-finger discounts for friends wanting to watch Victor Mature run around in a loincloth. The Strand, in other words, is a vital part of our past, if not of our lives today.

We seem to just go rent those tapes and disks now and stay home and watch the newer films when we feel like it, and that might be because we now appreciate being able to stop the action for an occasional bathroom break now and then.

Attendance dropped dramatically when home entertainment really hit a lick. But Mickey fought back. He tried the free popcorn route for a while. All he charged for was the butter. Attendance didn't really pick up, and the popcorn bill was ... well, appreciable if not staggering.

Mickey now thinks he has the answer. He bought a disk player thingie that works on a big screen. Then he bought some old movies and lowered the price.

The first night he did this was a triple header, and we all turned out to see our old heroes vanquish Nazis, solve the bank robbery in Cactus Gulch, and find out who really killed the big-city mayor. We paid too much for popcorn, but who cares?

The Strand lives on, even if there is more gray hair there than at a Percheron horse show. Besides, when was the last time you saw The Duke standing 15-feet tall?

Coffee always tastes perfect before daylight on the opening day of deer season, Dud Campbell thought as he sat in near-total darkness in his kitchen. It was Anita's first year as his wife in deer season, and he was extra quiet so as not to awaken her. Turning on a flashlight on the kitchen counter, he wrote:

Honey, I'll be up Pine Canyon, hunting up a feeder creek 1.4 miles to the right. The truck will be at the campground. Doc and Steve both know the area I'm hunting. I'll be back no later than 10 p.m. unless I call.

An hour later, Dud quietly got out of the pickup and left a note under the windshield wiper:

Hunting to the west between here and the ridge. Should be back here no later than 9 p.m.
Dud Campbell

Dud was sitting on a rock outcropping as the sun rose, feeling the warmth spread from inside out as another great day of anticipation came. He smiled, and then prayed. He always did during hunting season. His prayer wasn't wishing for success, but simply expressing gratitude for this special time. This was the success. Sitting here in the sun, hunting yet another year. An actual deer for the freezer is simply gravy on this feast.

After lunch, Dud decided to try a different location, so he returned to the pickup and left a different note. He got home about 9 p.m. and raved to Anita about the wonders of the day in the woods.

"You left me that note, Dud," she said, "but I don't even know where that is."

"No. But the sheriff's department does, and search and rescue knows, and both Doc and Steve know."

She still looked puzzled. "You're a good outdoorsman, though, aren't you?"

"Well, yes I am. That's why I left the notes. Anyone can twist an ankle or fall up there."

He smiled at her. "Hunters have an old saying, Honey. If you take crutches with you, you'll never break a leg."

It was Doc's idea, of course. That's what made it sing. That's why it took off in gales of laughter and fun.

He knew we needed the money for the children in our area who might be without warm clothes this winter, so he brainstormed among himself and came up with the golf tournament.

He went to Delbert McLain, who is our local chamber of commerce. Delbert's eyes lit up at the suggestion, but then suddenly clouded over with doubt.

"But Doc," Delbert said, "we don't have a golf course."

"Leave that to me, Delbert me lad. Leave that entirely to me."

And so our medical leprechaun talked to two farmers whose land adjoined each other, and after they quit laughing, they agreed.

Doc rounded up Dud and Herb Collins and laid out an 18-hole golf course in about an hour. They used steel t-posts for flags (with bandanas tied to the top) and dug a hole with a shovel. They put smaller flags at the tee-off spots, and there you go! An 18-hole golf course that was one hundred percent hazard.

No fairway, just hazard. Rocks and trees and Lewis Creek and the occasional cactus and yucca. Doc figures if you make it around all 18 holes without encountering a poisonous snake, you should get bonus points.

"This course," said Doc, "is so bad, everyone will want to play, because everyone will have a terrific excuse for having a terrible game."

The cattle were moved to safer locations before the tournament began, and enough money was raised to keep the kids warm this winter.

"Life," said Doc, "should be ridiculous and fun. So let's do this again next fall."

It was that magic time of morning for those of us at the Mule Barn; the time when we're so full of coffee we can't walk, and it's time to decide whether to order lunch there or go home. That's when Bert walked in. Kinda limped in, actually. He made his way over and sat down and turned his coffee cup right side up.

"I'm hurting boys," he said. "That's a fact. 'Course Maizie told me it was a fool thing to do, but you know how she is, so I did it anyway."

"What's that, Bert?"

"Grandfathering, that's what. But what the heck, guys, you gotta do it, don't you? I mean, we owe it to the kids to start them on the road ... yes, that straight and narrow road leading to a fulfilling future, filled with..."

"Bert," said Doc, "you get tattooed with a phonograph needle? Just tell us what happened."

"My granddaughter, Gina," he said. "She's eight now, you know, and she's been staying with us for a while. Well, she's the best girl you ever met, but it's hard to get her up on time. Seems like every other day she fools around and misses the school bus, and then we have to drive her to school. I just got tired of that, and figured I'd teach her a lesson.

"Well, she missed the bus again this morning and said, 'Grandpa, you'll have to take me to school.' And I said, 'OK, Honey, get your books.' So she got her little backpack with the books on and I walked her to school."

"All the way to school? How far is it from your farm?"

"Eight miles, boys. Eight very long miles."

He grinned. "Several times people stopped and offered us rides, but I just said no thanks, and explained that it was an object lesson. Gina just mumbled that she hated object lessons, but she kept walking. Walked all the way up the canyon and didn't sit down once."

"How about Grandpa?" Dud asked.

"He didn't sit down, either. Hey, how would it look?"

"No wonder you're tired, Bert."

"Well," he said, grinning. "I don't expect I'll ever need to do this again. I believe the lesson got learned just fine."

Old Jasper Blankenship went out to hunt deer the other day, the same way he's done for decades now. Deer season has changed a lot for

Jasper over the many years he's been at it. As a kid, he couldn't wait until he was old enough to get a license, because he wanted to bring a buck home to show his family. Not just any buck, either, but a big one.

As a young man, he wanted to see how many hunting seasons he could have in one year: duck, goose, quail, pheasant, deer, about anything that moved.

As a middle-aged man, he turned to the technology of hunting and wanted to learn about the newest gizmo that would make you quiet, make you invisible, make you irresistible to deer.

But things are different these days. Oh, Jasper still enjoys going through all the outdoor magazines and orders catalogs, and each year he buys some new gizmo that guarantees to bring home the meat. But he just chuckles at them, even as he orders them. Hunting, to him, means a reattachment to nature, a return to his roots. It is a time to see if his personal skills are still adequate. It is also a time to sit on a ridge and look around and appreciate what is there. And if what isn't there happens to be a deer, well, that's all right, too.

Venison isn't getting any easier to pack back to camp after all these many seasons, either. But there is something in the hunt, something in being allowed to silently stalk the nameless essence of fall, something in moving in near invisibility. There is *something*.

Sometimes it's just nice to go out there and see what happens.

There could be lots of reasons Martin chose to become the "crossing sergeant."

He's always kept to himself. His wife, too. Oh, there have been rumors that she may give Martin a hard time at home, but you know how rumors are.

Martin retired from the Field Ranch a while back after about 40 years. After that, we'd see him out walking or maybe fishing a little along Lewis Creek. Then one day in September, Martin found his new career as a crossing guard down next to the elementary school. He got a blaze orange vest, a paddle sign with "stop" on one side and "slow" on the other. And they gave him a whistle. Oh yes, *the whistle*. At first, when a child was spotted a block away, Martin would trot out to the middle of the intersection, blow his whistle, hold up his paddle and turn it around so everyone saw "stop," regardless of where you were. And we'd wait until some third-grader got safely to school.

Then we were waved on through. And with each wave of Martin's hand there was a blast on the whistle. Oh yes, *that whistle*.

The school sure picked the right guy for the job. If you want someone who can stand out there every morning in heat and rain and snow and spring winds, just look for an old cowboy. Martin took all his "tough lessons" ages ago.

The problem Martin was having, however, was that he had more time than children, and that led to his current traffic-control methods. He watches carefully, and if a car is coming from a right angle, he steps out and blows the whistle and stops us. And if the car slows, Martin waves him on whether he wants to go that way or not. And that's when there aren't any kids around.

But no one complains. He's there early, he'd stop a train to let kids cross the street, and he works for free. So what's a few whistle blasts and marching orders among friends?

You have to admire professionalism wherever it is found.

"Moon's getting big," Dud said over coffee the other day.

"Sure is," said Herb Collins.

"Time to go after The Ghost again."

"Tomorrow night?"

"I'll be there," said Dud.

The Ghost, hereabouts, is a raccoon. He lives along Lewis Creek and is a wily old rascal. We love going coonhunting here, but the way we do it is a bit different than they do it other places. Since we don't have a lot of water around us, as they do in some areas, we don't have a lot of 'coons, either. So we conserve the 'coons, but not the fun. We throw 'em back when we're done.

So we take these beautiful fall and winter nights, put on several layers of longjohns, and turn the hounds out along the creek. Sometimes the dogs strike a 'coon track and put the 'coon up the tree quickly. Then we tell the dogs how wonderful they are, hook the dogs to leashes, and drag them back to the truck. It's hunting's answer to catch-and-release. The coons stay in the tree until we're gone and then go back to making the nights more interesting.

But not The Ghost. The Ghost is a big male, or boar. We've treed him 139 more than a dozen times now, and then he discovered this was kinda fun. So now he waits in a one-acre patch of trees. Waits for the dogs. And when they catch his scent, he takes those dogs through farmyards, across busy streets, even past the dog pound. He does everything he can to shake them off his trail, and it works. The dogs haven't treed him in three years now. It the dogs get smart to his ways and put too much pressure on him, he swims the river.

So Dud and Herb will try The Ghost again tomorrow. Will the dogs put him up a tree this time? Don't bet on it.

Some of the earlier knights of the coffee table arrived just before daylight, flipping their cups to the upright and fillable positions, and were joined quickly by Dewey, which is an unusual occurrence. Doc was the only one of us downwind from Dewey, and we watched to see if any fainting took place, but evidently Dewey had not yet begun his job of transferring soil nutrients from the dairies to people's yards.

"How's it going, Dewey?" Dud said. We all like Dewey.

"Finer'n frog hair, Dud. My shoulder's in shape for a shovel and I'm sure gonna shovel…"

"Well, yes you are," Doc said, quickly.

"Dewey's an interesting name," Dud said. "Was your mother … dewy eyed when you were born?"

"That's D-E-W-Y. My name has the extra e in it. Actually, I was named for a famous man."

We sipped over that one for a minute.

"Thomas E. Dewey!" shouted Doc. "Governor of New York. Candidate for President. Your mother was a Republican, right?"

"Uh, no … not him, I'm afraid."

"I know …" said Steve. "Admiral Dewey. Whats-his-name … George. George Dewey of the Spanish-American War! Your dad was a fan of the Navy."

"Well, not exactly," Dewey said, although privately he thought that would've been a good guy to be named for.

"Well?" said Doc. "I've run out of Deweys. Who was it?"

"Melvil."

"Who?"

"Melvil Dewey," Dewey said. "You know … Dewey Decimal System?

My mom was a librarian."

When Pop Walker sneaked out the kitchen door the other day, it affected all of us. He's been a resident of the Rest of Your Life retirement home for several years now.

He still remembers who said what during combat in Europe, but has a hard time remembering if he's had breakfast.

The call went out down at the sheriff's office around 10 p.m. that Pop had slipped through enemy lines, meaning the kitchen staff, and was on the loose. One of the deputies called Doc, who was a friend of his since forever, and Doc alerted the rest of us.

Pop is one of our own, of course. A couple of years ago, he took his coffee black and his philosophy straight at the philosophy counter at the Mule Barn.

It was cold, and they found his heavy coat still in his room, so this wasn't good.

The deputies checked out the interstate and volunteers hit the all-night diners to see if he'd checked in there. No luck.

The cook at the home was crying, and she said Pop had been talking about going to see his buddy, Jasper, again, and did we know someone named Jasper?

Sure. Jasper Blankenship, up at the cabin in the mountains. When we heard this, the hunt actually took more form. Two guys started up at Jasper's place and worked down the road. Steve and Dud both went horseback and started from the edge of town.

Steve found him. Pop was sitting and shivering under a tree high up on a ridge. Steve used the cell phone to let us know he was all right, then built a fire and wrapped a blanket around Pop.

Pop wouldn't go back until Steve told him Jasper was down at the home, waiting for him. And Steve let him ride in the saddle, too. But before that happened, Steve ducked off behind a rock and made another phone call, to be sure Jasper would be there.

Two hours later, everyone had coffee and doughnuts back at the home, and they fixed the lock on the kitchen door. We have to be careful with those who have problems. We can't afford to lose beautiful people like Pop.

She shouldn't have asked Herb to do it. We all knew that, but there's this new teacher down at the elementary school, and she wasn't familiar with Herb's reputation. All she had heard, from one of the Johnson kids, was that Mr. Collins, who lived on their street, was a nice guy and raised bees and fishing worms.

What the teacher hadn't heard was that our dear Mr. Collins was a retired businessman who happened to be a frustrated stand-up comic, as well. Consequently, she invited Herb to come to Career Day and speak to her second graders about the joys and pitfalls of raising bees and worms.

Herb wore his white bee suit to school ... with a necktie. He brought a can of worms with him, and several bees in a glass jar with a lid on it and some holes poked in the lid.

"These are honey bees, kids," he said. "Can anyone tell me why we raise them?"

Hands flew up.

"To get honey!"

"Well, yes," Herb said. "How about another reason?"

"To pollinate apple orchards!"

"Well, that, too," Herb said. "But what's the main reason?"

Silence.

"The truth is we brush them ... very carefully ... to get bee wool so we can make sweaters."

One hand raised slowly.

"But Mr. Collins, won't they sting us?"

"That's why you have to brush them when they're asleep, usually between midnight and four in the morning."

The teacher looked perplexed.

"Mr. Collins, I've never heard of bee wool. Can you tell us what it is, exactly?"

"Certainly. It's very fine, of course, but it is still one step below 'A' wool."

Then Herb dampened a wash cloth he'd brought with him, and opened his can of worms. Picking a worm out of the earth, he held it up and watched it wiggle, then picked up the wash cloth.

"Now kids," Herb said, "it's time you learned about the importance of keeping your worms clean."

Whenever my lack of mechanical prowess threatens to surface, I sure miss the solenoid. It was always there for us, lurking under the hood somewhere, and always – *always* – it was waiting to malfunction. It was handy, every mechanic knew where it was - like tonsils - and it had a great name. Solenoid - like asteroid and paranoid and hemorrhoid.

In the old days, b.c.c. (before car computers), the solenoid was a little whatchit that was in the engine area and without it you couldn't make the car go. And that's an important thing for those of us who are mechanically impaired to know.

I asked Vince down at the gas station gun shop about solenoids and why we don't hear about them any more. "Oh, they're still in there," he said, "but now they're a part of the starter and everything is run by a computer, so you don't see them separately any more."

Vince began selling guns at the gas station several years ago so he could combine his two great loves: gasoline and gun powder. The place has never been held up.

So the solenoid is still around, reducing current from the battery and closing little doodiddles inside the thingie-things, but it isn't separate any more. This is a terrible blow to guys like me. The solenoid, bless it, saw a long career as the whipping boy of ignorance. In those days, if the car didn't start, you'd raise the hood, start tapping on various parts with a screwdriver, and wait for someone to come by and take pity on you.

"Not starting?" the mechanically-inclined angel of mercy would say.

And then we would look semi-philosophical and reply. "Can't get it going. Think it might be the solenoid."

This gave us a graceful way out of just looking stupid. What are we supposed to say these days? My car's gone off-line?

Sure do miss that solenoid.

You know, it isn't always easy being a crossing guard for the kids. It especially isn't easy when you're an old crossing guard, and Martin is old. This isn't meant as a slight, because there are few people around here who don't treasure Martin for the many years he's spent ushering kids across the intersection at the school since he retired from the ranch work. It's

143

just a fact, being old means extra work trying to keep up with trends and fads and technology.

"The first problem I had," said Martin, "was those cell phone thingies. You know ... the ones that stick in your ear and make you look like a Martian with an earring? Man oh man, the first few times I saw kids using those I thought the world was coming to an end. I'd stop the cars for a kid and he'd walk across the street, talking to himself. I thought them kids were nuts, you know? Then they told me they were on the phone. I still have a hard time getting used to them.

"But this latest doo-lolly they have," he says, "gives me the fantods. They got these sneakers now ... maybe you seen 'em ... got these little wheels in 'em. Yeah, like half a roller skate. Well, those kids come along and I go to stop traffic and before I can do that, you know, these little turkeys sit back on their heels and go sailing across the street on them wheels. They're too fast for me now."

He shook his head. "Ain't safe, you know. Just ain't safe."

When Bob Garcia removed that old mossyhorn mount from its place over the fireplace, we were a bit confused. That huge buck had been his pride and joy for more than 30 years. But Bob put it back in his office, behind the kitchen. The spot of honor over the fireplace now belongs to a young forked-horn buck, the one he took last year on the other side of the hayfield. It's the kind of buck you expect to get for your first buck, and not really the kind of buck you honor like that after a lifetime spent hunting in the autumn woods.

Bob just said it was a special buck, and he smiled.

Bob heard the deer before he saw him, and he got ready. He looked to the sound of the deer and checked what was on the other side of the animal. A large dirt bank. That's safe enough. Can't have that old .45–70 slug sailing around the country.

Bob felt the breeze coming right to his face, slightly chilling his nose, and carrying with it the promise of a crisp fall later on. These days still held some late summer heat. The wind was right, and he wore dull clothing, he had a clear shot with a safe backdrop. There was nothing to do now but wait.

Then the little forked-horn buck stepped out. It would never replace the huge buck Bob took years back, but it was a good eating deer and the situation was right, so he aimed carefully and shot.

The sound of the massive cartridge going off started the snake at his feet rattling. Bob jumped back out of danger and finished the snake. Another step forward ... just one more step.

The taxidermist was surprised when Bob told him he wanted a really nice mount of what was, to all other eyes, a fairly routine meat deer. But he promised to give the buck the full treatment.

It hangs over the fireplace now.

When outdoorsmen ask him about that deer, Bob just says it is a special buck, and he smiles.

"You see that sunset last night?" Steve said. "Now that was a honey."

"I'll say," said Doc. "You know, with Thanksgiving almost on us, I have to tell you I'm very thankful for sunsets like that one."

Those of us who don't live in the big cities tend to be thankful for different things than those who may live in stucco cliff dwellings. We tend to look at the natural blessings more than the manmade ones. Our gratitude extends past not having our teenager go to jail, or for the raise we just got at the factory. Our favorite ball team can win or lose on its own without our having to look for Divine Intervention, usually. We tend to be grateful for other things, like calves in the spring, and how clean they look before they discover mud.

We are deeply grateful that tasty rabbits arrive in large litters, and bears don't. When we think about it, we are thankful that we get eggs from hens and not from rattlesnakes, as checking the rattler house each morning could get 'way too exciting.

When you consider that quills come on porcupines and not deer, it gives us pause for praise, and we're happy that it's skunks who carry scent glands and not squirrels.

We are thankful, too, that hurricanes and tornadoes only happen in warm weather. It's bad enough to lose the barn without being chill-factored to death while it's happening.

"Turkeys," Dud said, sipping his coffee.

"What?"

"I'm thankful turkeys are stupid. Ever looked in a turkey's eyes? Not only is no one home, but there was a mass evacuation sometime during the Eisenhower Administration. A turkey has just enough brains to operate his heart and lungs."

"You're thankful for that?" Doc said.

"Sure," said Dud. "If turkeys had been given the rudimentary intelligence of a garden snail, we might be forced to eat sheep on Thanksgiving."

"Teak surfing," Doc said, raising his head from the paper. "That tears it. Now they've outlawed teak surfing."

We looked at Doc and wondered how late he'd been up the night before.

"You know," Doc said, "teak surfing, the great sport in Oregon? Well, here's a story about it. It seems that idiots in Oregon grab hold of the back of speedboats and get dragged along on their feet at high speeds in the ocean, and now they've outlawed it, because the teak surfers inhale fumes from the motor and get goofy."

"Never heard of it," Dud said.

"And I guess you never will again," Doc said. "It's been outlawed."

"It's like hooky-bob," said Bert. "The dumb kids up north play hooky-bob in the winter. They hide until a car pulls up to a stop sign, then they sneak out from the bushes, grab hold of the back bumper and squat down. When the car starts up, they slide along on the snow-covered road until they get going about 30 miles an hour, then let go and see how far they can slide until some other car puts them in the hospital."

"Well," said Steve, "I feel a little left out because I didn't bob any hookies or surf any teaks."

"You just haven't lived right, Steve," said Doc, laughing.

"That's right," said the tall cowboy. "About the only thing I did as a kid was pasture surfing."

We looked at him. "Pasture surfing?"

"When I was a little fella, my dad got a new rope, and naturally the new rope needed breaking in, so I roped old Brownie with it, our Brown Swiss milk cow? When Brownie felt that loop come tight, she decided to see if an old milk cow could run real fast around her pasture with a dumb kid being dragged behind her."

"And?"

"The answer was yes."

"Did the rope get broken in?" Doc asked.

"Sure did," Steve said, grinning. "And so did the seat of my pants."

"Hey Bert!" we all said, cheerfully, as our pal joined us at the Mule Barn truck stop's philosophy counter.

Bert just groaned, flipped over his coffee mug, and sank his head into his hands.

"Bad news?" Steve asked.

Bert groaned and shook his head.

"Tax trouble?" ventured Doc.

More shaking of the head.

"My stars," said Dud, "I'll bet Maizie's left him and run off with a French hairdresser!"

Even Bert had to chuckle at that one.

"Worse, guys," he said. "Much worse."

We all looked at him.

"I got an official notice in my mailbox from the U.S. Government of Postal Service," Bert said. "My mailbox has been condemned."

"No!" shouted the chorus.

"It's a fact," he said, nodding. "Now boys, you know I did my time in the service, right? And I pay my taxes whether I want to or not. I even help old ladies across the street."

"That's right," said Doc. "Whether they want to cross or not."

"We're with you, Bert," said Steve.

"And for all this patriotism, what do I get? *Condemned!*"

"That about tears it all right," said Steve. "This country was a wonderful experiment in liberty while it lasted, but when they condemn a man's mailbox…"

"Can you appeal this to a higher court, Bert?"

"No chance. I've been given orders by a uniformed agent of the federal government that I have to fasten it so it isn't wobbly."

"Or ….?"

"Or they won't bring me any more offers to give me credit cards or tell me how much round steak is down at the market, or …"

"Say no more, Bert," said Doc. "We'll all go help you fix it. Right guys?"

"Right!"

"Right after coffee…."

Steve slowly saddled his horse, Snort, and climbed stiffly aboard in the cold snap of morning. He pulled his hat down a little lower and pulled the wild rag up to cover his nose and mouth from the morning chill.

How many mornings had he done this?

As Snort trotted out into the meadows of the hills surrounding our valley, he looked with perked ears for cattle. That's what Snort does for a living. Those ears worked back and forth like radar, searching through trees and behind logs for the tell-tale movement or color of range cattle.

And Steve just grinned. How many horses has he ridden on a morning like this? A hundred? Well, fifty, anyway. And the mornings all stay the same in his memory even if he doesn't stay the same. On a morning like this, his daily dose of "cowboyitis" lets itself be felt. That aching hip? Oh, he remembers when that colt dumped him into the rockpile, putting him on crutches for two months.

The shoulder ache? Too many years with a rope in his hands.

But he also knows when the fall sun gets a little higher, he'll stretch and suddenly get younger. His gray mustache will, in his mind, turn brown again, and once more that young cowboy who terrorized stray cattle so many years ago will come back to life.

He began kicking cows out and heading them back to the home pasture, and both he and Snort watched and waited for that one rogue that would make the morning complete.

It was a black baldy cow who made a dash for the high-ups and Steve and Snort were flying through trees and over rock piles and finally headed her and turned her back with the others. A 19-year-old cowboy couldn't have done it any better.

Steve smiled and reached down to pat ol' Snort on the neck.

Thanksgiving can mean more than turkey and cranberry sauce.

The last of the geese went by the other day. The late ones. The big dark geese. Headed south noisily.

I used to envy them, somehow. They go down there to the warm coastal areas where the jacks swim and the nights are chilly but livable this time of year. If they're especially sensitive geese, they'll keep going until there are mangoes and palm trees and the language of the people is Spanish.

But they cross over here in their long, languorous vees, and all we can do is look up and wonder what our lives would be like if we could go along. To fly over the farms and valleys, to coast along on the rising thermals, to sail down the long way to warmth and sand and comfort, how nice it might be.

But if we did that, we'd miss the snow, and the fire in the fireplace when the work was done in the evening. We'd miss how the snowy world looks just at dusk when the snow is an alpenglow orange and tells us secrets it has saved for us all these years.

If we went to the winter feeding grounds, we wouldn't be able to appreciate how splendid the spring will be with the basking rays of sun on our necks and the swelling of the buds in the fruit trees. To truly appreciate warmth, we must first get cold, and that's evidently a part of our lives that the geese won't ever get to share.

Of course, they seem quite content to sail on down the southern winds to the warm places, leaving us to wrap ourselves tighter in thicker clothes and dream of sandy beaches and snorkels. Have a good winter, geese. Eat a crab or two for me. You see, I'll be here for you to honk at when you head north again in the spring. I'll be right here, living in the same place. Cold or hot, windy or still, my world and my responsibilities are here, and I'll be right here taking care of them.

It's my way of doing things, and I'm used to it.

Winter

The cold has set in and covered the summer things. But even as it buries some of our treasures, it creates others: reading by the fire, watching the lace filigree of bare branches against a setting sun and the warmth and laughter and food of unforgettable holidays.
And, if we should find time to look within ourselves with some serious questions, that's okay too. Winter's like that.

There is a nighttime sweetness and hope that hovers over us this time of year here at home. This is a time for summing up and looking ahead … and a time for dreams.

And at night… ah, that's the time, isn't it? Outside it's dark, December dark, and we're inside and warm and cocooned up. The cold makes our world shrink, especially at night.

But we have our dreams.

For Janice Thomas, our art teacher at the high school, it's that painting she's planning. She makes starts at it, from time to time, but she's wise enough to know she isn't good enough to paint it yet. She paints other things well, but that one … it has to be perfect. It will be the painting of a lifetime, she knows.

Doc will drift off to sleep tonight thinking about that new fly rod. He has half a dozen, of course, that will take about any weight line, and let him catch anything from mouse to moose. But even the most expensive rod isn't what he dreams of. This year, for Christmas, he's giving himself a rod-builder's jig, and he will make his own rod from a Sage blank. That will be the one. It will have his own wrappings and he'll put the ferrules on it himself. He'll be able to feel the fish *breathe* with this one. It will be true and wonderful and last forever.

For cowboy Steve, the December dream is always the same: staying in that little cabin. The one with a turret and a corral. And hearing ol' Snort happily eating out there in the corral. And exploring. Time enough to explore those mountains with Snort.

There is a nighttime sweetness and hope that hovers over us this time of year. Here's to dreams.

It's Tuesday afternoon at two, which means Clarice Devon is on her way to the Curl Up 'N Dye beauty salon. It's like the sun coming up or the price of bread increasing. Tuesday. Two. Clarice.

"Clarice!" yells Fran. "Ready to be beautiful?"

"Sure," she said. "I like attempting the impossible."

Clarice Devon is one of our angels. She's one of the few people in town who will tolerate old people and shut ins, and she not only takes care of them, but seems to relish it as well.

During the rinse, Fran asks her if she's the one taking care of Mr. Gavin since his stroke. Clarice nods.

"So what's he like to work with these days?"

"It's a now-and-then situation," Clarice says. "You know ... now and then?"

"I don't understand. You mean it's part time?"

"Nope. Full time. But it's now and then."

Fran looked puzzled.

Clarice laughed. "It's like this," she said, imitating old Mr. Gavin's voice. "*Now*, when you finish getting me my tea, I'd like a custard, but I'd like it in a glass bowl. A small glass bowl. *Then* I want you to call and see if my pills are ready. *Now* if they are, could you pick them up? *Then*, while you're there, I want to try that toothpaste they talk about on television."

Fran laughed. "Now and then, huh?"

"Now and then," Clarice said, smiling as she was attacked by curlers.

Someday it would be interesting if social scientists would spend some of that grant money on finding out how some good things get started, as well as discovering sources of pestilence and plague.

It shouldn't be all that difficult. For example, the Cookie Thing wasn't all that hard to figure out.

The Cookie Thing, we concluded, began with old Jasper Blankenship. He came down from his cabin at the diggin's and brought with him an entire half pillowcase of cookies. He had found the recipe in one of those 30-year-old magazines he has up there, and since the snow was too deep to do anything else, he baked cookies.

Jasper walked into the Soup 'R Market and handed a cookie to Annette. "We don't often get to say how much we appreciate each other, Annette," the old man said, "so here ... have a cookie."

She thanked him and talked about it for the rest of the day.

Jasper found Doc walking toward the Mule Barn and his daily cup of coffee and handed him a cookie, too.

"Doc ... the way you took care of that ... little problem of mine ... well, I want you to know how much I appreciate it. Here, have a cookie."

Before the day was over and Jasper headed back to the diggin's, half the valley had been cookied, and the other half wished they had. Carla Martinez had been cookied and decided to carry on the tradition, so she whipped up a batch of *biscochitos* and began passing them out, along with compliments.

153

Bert asked Maizie to make a batch of chocolate chip cookies, his particular favorite, and handed them out, along with compliments. Mickey Baker had store-bought cookies to hand out two nights later at the ticket booth at The Strand, where a Randolph Scott Western was playing for the first time in 60 years. Each cookie came with a compliment, too. This seems to be the most important element of Jasper's new valley tradition.

Cookies and compliments. Not a bad way to say I love you.

It might have been the winter doldrums that did it. You can never be sure of these things. It's just that ... well, Doc is one of those guys who can't stand to see anyone bored. He claims it's bad for their inner chemistry, and since he has more initials after his name than anyone else in town, we tend to listen to him.

When it happened, we in the inner circle of the world dilemma think tank down at the Mule Barn truck stop thought back on what Doc had said a year ago when the temperature dropped, along with everyone's spirits.

"In weather like this," Doc pronounced, stirring sugar into his cup, "a real American would come up with a great hoax."

Those of us sitting at the philosophy counter that morning just nodded, even though we didn't have a clue. No one wanted to admit it, you see.

When the Valley Weekly Miracle hit the street yesterday, we bought one to see how much the editor dared to print, as always, but there in the classifieds was this:

LOST – One gray squirrel, fluffy tail, two years old. Answers to "Chipper." $5.25 reward. Call Doc.

The paper was passed down the counter and we all looked at Doc after we read it. He was smirking as only Doc can smirk.

"Doc," Steve said, tentatively, "would this be the same imaginary squirrel that was kidnapped and held for ransom last year?"

"The very same," Doc said. "I named him Chipper."

"But he's imaginary, right?"

"The very best kind."

"Why?"

154 "Imaginary squirrels don't bite, don't have to be fed, and you never

have to clean up after them," he said. "And a real squirrel will eat the leg off a coffee table."

He grinned. "Besides, I've always wanted an imaginary squirrel."

After we laughed, Dud said, "And what if someone finds a squirrel and brings him to you?"

"Dudley," he said, "I figure it's worth $5.25 to get a squirrel, which would be hibernating this time of year, of course, and then to turn it loose. Besides, I'll make more money than that just stitching up the squirrel catcher's hand."

When the new college opened in the next town – a somewhat larger town than ours – our folks began wondering if making the 30-minute drive to class would be worth it.

Dud was the first to figure out that it was.

"Boys," he said, sitting at the Mule Barn philosophy counter and flipping his cup upright with one poetic motion, "I'm signed up over at J.H.T.. I'm going to get me an education."

"That's great, Dud," said his mentor and straight man, Doc. "What are you taking?"

"Just one class to start out, Doc," Dud said. "Thought I'd kinda e-e-e-ease into it, you know. I'm taking functional literacy. We're going to study words and their meanings."

"I thought you did that in high school. Maybe even in grammar school?"

"Right, Doc. But this is college, you know. We're going to take functional literacy to a higher plane!"

When Jerry Hat-Trick Junior College recently opened its doors, it attracted a great deal of attention. Not only was it the first privately-endowed junior college in the country, but it was named for its benefactor, the famous retired hockey player. It had always been Jerry's dream, he told the world, to bring about a greater appreciation for the associate in arts degree. To do this, he paid educators to meet in think tanks all over the county and come up with classes that were "outside the box."

Jerry did well in hockey, naturally, but endowing a two-year institution of semi-higher learning became possible only after he married the heiress to a pork-belly fortune. You might call that "functional matrimony."

So J.H.T. J.C. was born, having innovative classes like "Pruning for the New Millenium," "Creative Sword Swallowing," and "First-Strike Self Defense."

It got some of the rest of us considering a return to the halls of Virginia creeper for a tune-up. After all, as charter members of the Mule Barn truck stop's world dilemma think tank, it's our duty to stay on the cutting edge.

When Steve and Dud got up to go get a paper, it left just Doc and Bert sitting at the philosophy counter of the Mule Barn truck stop. Bert turned his head and smirked a little, being careful not to let Doc see him. Doc also didn't see Dud outside, punching in a number on his cell phone while Steve stood by as a cheerleader.

"Doc," said Loretta, from the cash register, "phone call for you, Hon."

"Here? Okay..." Doc walked over and picked up the phone.

"This here Doc?" said the caller. "The Doc what lost his squirrel?"

"Uh ..." Doc looked around for help. There was none. "Yes. Yes it is."

"Found your dang squirrel here, Doc. That reward thing still good?"

"Well ... yes."

"Five dollars and a quarter, right? Now is that cash or check? I don't take no checks."

Doc is looking all around and looks wilderness-type lost. "Cash I guess."

"Only thing is, Doc. Need to be sure this is your squirrel, right? So can you describe him for me?"

"He's ... gray."

"All gray squirrels are gray, now, ain't that right? How about any distinguishing marks? Tattoos?"

"No tattoos."

"So far so good. Now you said in the ad his name is Chipper. Well, I called him Chipper and the son of a gun bit me."

"He did?"

"What I mean to ask here, Doc, is did you and your squirrel get along? No squirrel problems? He looks like he needs a square meal to me. You feed him good?"

"What?"

"You know … like Squirrel Chow free choice, or did you put him on a nut ration? I mean, he ate like there was no tomorrow. Dang near ate up the whole five dollars and a quarter reward money in squirrel food."

Steve and Dud walked back into the café, then, with the cell phone still at Dud's ear, and the laughing began.

"You were right all along, Doc," said Bert. "In winter, everyone can use a good hoax."

Doc paid for the coffee.

It's natural to mumble nasty things about the cold weather. We all do it from time to time. But even the cold has its merits.

One big plus is that it makes fireplaces a reasonable addition to our lives. In cold weather, we can build a fire in our home with a clear conscience. This is something that doesn't translate well to summer heat, but when it's cold, here comes the fire.

Strange, isn't it, our love affair with a fireplace? Makes absolutely no sense. Today, we can make houses so impervious to cold that every time we light a candle, the temperature goes up ten degrees. So what do we do? We cut a hole in this sealed anti-cold unit so we can sit and look at the flames, the way our ancestors have done since they learned to walk upright and invented kindling.

But we don't care. We'll spend a lot of extra money to buy a house with a fireplace, and not think a thing about it. Because this fireplace is the spiritual center of a home, as it's always been. It's the gathering place. It's the place to read, to learn, to meet and tell stories. It's the core of our universe. The fireplace – and those waiting for us there – is what we dream about when we're miles from home in the woods or desert. It warms us, inside and out, cooks our food, and answers our questions.

Questions? Sure.

When the fire's burning low, and you can just see the little blue lickem flames curling around the glowing embers late at night, and when we've about talked out the day's adventures, we can look at those embers and find answers to questions we didn't even know we had. And we feel sorry for people who don't have these advantages.

Sarah McKinley has a real problem this time of year. Sarah owns and runs (and is the only one there) at Read Me Now bookstore. Since this is the only bookstore for about 30 miles, you'd figure its success would be a slam dunk, but it doesn't work this time of year.

"During the holidays," she says, "most bookstores make a bundle from women buying cookbooks."

But that isn't so here.

"I believe it's a fem-cho thing," Sarah says. "You know ... the women's version of macho," she explains. We won't find that particular word in any dictionary, she said, but if we'd care to look, she'd be glad to sell us one.

"Fem-cho is the art of being just a bit more woman than the next girl," Sarah says. "You know how it is when a woman's pregnant, right? Every old biddie in town has to tell this poor woman horror stories of when she was giving birth, about a hundred years ago.

"'Women have it easy today,' they say. 'Why, when I was having my children, it was like being torn apart by a bulldozer wrapped in barbed wire!'"

Sarah says this starts a pain auction that carries on until the poor pregnant woman wishes she'd never even considered having children. Each woman who tosses chips into the conversation ups the ante on pain and misery just enough to keep the conversation heading for the total destruction of all female parts.

"It's that way with my cookbooks here, too," Sarah says. "We have these new low-carb cookbooks and everything ... and you can't tell me there aren't plenty of us who could stand to lose a few pounds ... but they won't buy them. I don't care if they're the worst cook in the county. If they are seen buying a cookbook, it's an admission of defeat, a very real confession that she isn't as much woman as the other cooks in the area."

Sarah grinned. "And let's face it, there are some cooks around here who could use some new recipes!"

Why are the winter mornings so heartbreakingly special? They're sure cold, at least around here. And with the snow you'd think they'd be white, too. But they aren't, are they?

In the morning there is a tinge, a golden ... no a yellowish cast to the snow, the sky, and the trees. It is more like those catalog pictures of yellow diamonds. You know… the diamonds we don't really want because the ladies don't want anything but the clear diamonds, but the ones that look more interesting because there's some color there?

If men bought diamonds for themselves, we'd probably go for the yellow ones, because they'd remind us, even in the broiling heat of summer, that a morning in January has a yellow-diamond cast to it.

And the evenings are special, too.

When the sun starts to set, the snow and the sky and the trees take on that glow that is a combination of orange and pink. It's the singular color of winter dusk and makes us want to paint the walls of a cabin that color to remind us of the endings of winter days. It's the color that's so pretty we don't even talk about it with other people because it would sound kinda silly. In Alaska, they call it "alpenglow." It's as good a name as any.

Isn't it strange how these days that are supposed to be white and gray and dull and depressing are still able to give us these two delicious colors we can tuck away in our memories and trot out when we need them?

Let's hope we can give each other special little memories this month that we can use when we need them, too. Seems like the right thing to do.

It was Herb who first saw Janice Thomas, the art teacher, come in.

"She's putting something up on the bulletin board," Herb said.

"Wonder what it says," said Doc.

"Might be something from school," Herb said.

Steve is of a more practical way of thinking. "You ever thought about going over there and seeing what it is?"

Steve got up and walked over and read the poster. He came back.

"It's an art show," Steve said. "For anyone who wants to enter."

"Haven't had an art show here in a long time."

"Those city guys who moved in the Johnson place, remember?"

"That was an art show?"

"Maybe."

"You know," Dud said, "there's more than one way to do art. You take Jim Kennedy now. The way he can pick up a little stick with his backhoe. How many people can do that? I think that's a kind of art."

"You're right, Dud," said Herb. "You ever watch Grant when he's fly

159

fishing?"

The members of the Mule Barn truck stop's philosophy counter and world-dilemma think tank nodded in agreement.

"Poetry, that is," said Doc.

"Dang near magic, to my mind," said Steve.

"How about the cream gravy here at the Mule Barn?" said Dud. "I don't know what they put in it, but you could eat a cardboard box if it had that gravy on it."

"I've never had better."

"Then there's Steve," said Doc.

"Me?" said the cowboy.

"You boys ever see anyone put a better rein on a horse than Steve?"

Steve blushed. "Now come on!"

"It's true, Steve."

"That," said Doc, "is art, too. Maybe art, maybe something like ballet almost, the way a horse moves when Steve's trained him."

"I guess there's more than one kind of art in the world," said Herb, "and I guess I personally know some artists."

There was Carla Martinez the other day, heaving a large pork butt onto the check-out counter down at the Soup 'R Market. Next from the depths of her basket came bag after bag of *masa harina*. This being winter, this means only one thing: it's tamale time!

So I said the obvious, of course. "Tamale time, Carla?"

"You know I make tamales for my family every winter. Tomorrow's the big day. My aunt's coming over to help, and maybe one of my granddaughters. We like to do it together, you know. It doesn't make sense to make just a few, so we all get together and really get tamale-ing around here. It's so nice. We've been doing it so long we each know our own jobs. There's the boiling and the wrapping and all the stuff that goes with it."

She grinned as spice after spice followed the *masa* onto the counter.

"It's traditional in our family, of course," she said, "but now there's something new."

"New?"

"Oh yes. My daughter, Gloria. Married that guy from San Francisco, you know? He is one of these nutrition student guys. Says it's bad to eat anything that ever had blood pressure, you know? He's one of these guys who thinks he's hurting his hair every time he goes to the barber shop, so he just doesn't. And my Gloria, she is doing the same thing he is. You know, running 50 miles before breakfast, drinking tea that isn't even brown, living on fruit and broccoli."

She tsk-tsk-ed and smiled. "So now," she said, "Gloria started in on my tamales. 'Make them with tofu, Mama'" Carla mimicked. "Tofu! You know what that is? Bean slime. Make tamales out of that? Hey, I make a couple out of turkey and if they don't like turkey, they just don't get any, I guess."

She looked disgusted. "You know what it is, don't you? Tofu tamales? It's un-American!"

There is a payoff, Doc told us, for getting the aches and pains of old age. Doc should know. We have it on good authority that he is actually older than a flat, brown rock.

"A payoff?" Steve said. Steve's an old cowpuncher who has collected hurt places for a long time now. He kinda wriggled around, reliving in two seconds' time two buck offs in the rocks, one horn wound from a nasty mama cow and a groin kick from a bronc mule.

"Sure," said Doc, in his usual cheerful way. "You get gray hair, or maybe kinda bald like ol' Steve here, and you develop wisdom, which we all know just means you know not to argue with your wife, right? So then what happens? Your grandchildren think you have all the answers."

"So you have to help them with homework?" Dud said.

"Naw, not a bit. What I mean is, you have your grandchildren all primed for some real Olympic-style embarrassment."

Doc leaned over conspiratorially. "I *live* to embarrass my grandchildren."

We had a good laugh, but Bert wanted specifics.

"With me," Doc said, "it's dancing. You see, they are all teenagers now, and therefore they are cool and know everything, and the world couldn't turn without them. So when their friends come over and they crank that stereo up to where it's killing the neighbor's geraniums, I ask them just once to turn it down."

"Takes me a lot more than once," Bert said. "I swear those kids are hard of hearing."

"But do you dance for them?" Doc asked. "You see, if they don't turn it down, I kinda totter to my feet and start what the kids call the Grandpa Boogie. I mean I shake it like an Egyptian pharaoh. I wiggle and jiggle and stick out my chin like this ... and sort of thrust myself around the floor until one of them dashes over and shuts off the music. Then I go sit down and read the paper again. The first couple of times I did that, the kids got me to one side and begged me never to do that again. I guess they were just jealous of my moves. Well, I hated to show them up in front of their friends, seeing as how I could dance better than they could, but the music was too loud. I tell them when the music gets more than just kinda regular, I can't help myself and dance fever hits me like a sledgehammer."

"So," Steve said, "how did you do it? I mean, show us, OK?"

So Doc stood up and went into spasms, twitches and slides that had the whole coffee shop cracking up, and people didn't know whether to applaud or call the paramedics.

"The really great thing," said Doc, sitting back down, out of breath, with his coffee, "is that these kids think they invented being cool. And I blind-sided them with great mo-o-o-o-ves! I showed them a slink or two.

"And you'd be surprised how much quieter it is when they come over these days."

Leave it to Janice. She hasn't been the valley's most innovative art teacher since the invention of dirt for nothing, you know.

It seems like every year or so, Janice Thomas comes up with some new idea to get the community involved in the art scene. She's gone so far as to invite several well-known artists from the city to come and give demonstrations here. It didn't do anything for the high school kids who were her actual students, but it did stir the artistic enthusiasm of some older folks who shouldn't be allowed near pigments.

So when Janice once again waltzed into the Mule Barn coffee shop and tacked up a poster, we almost had a foot race to check it out.

This year, she's having a sale and show of her students' work, but with a difference.

"The way I see it," she said, "these kids need some Christmas money, right?"

Coffee-sipping nods all around.

"And they need to take pride in their art work, too," she said. "So I kinda put it all together and came up with the 'Faces of Love' Christmas art show."

"Faces of Love?" said Dud.

"Oh yeah," Janice said, smiling. "You see, the paintings are all portraits of people the students love. You know, Mom and Dad, grandparents, the guy down the street who volunteers at band practice, that kind of thing."

"Sounds good," Doc said.

"And nothing at the art show will cost more than ten bucks. I figure we'll sell all of them, too."

"You sound pretty sure of that," said Doc. "Are they that good?"

"Frankly no," Janice said. "But hey, it's Christmas and they're only ten bucks."

"Still, selling all of them will be quite a trick," Doc said.

"Not really," Janice said. "I have a secret weapon."

We looked at her.

"I got the Valley Weekly Miracle to promise they'd print whatever portraits didn't sell."

Doc laughed and slapped his knee. "That's great! That oughta get 'em all right. Those poor folks don't have a chance."

"Wait until you see the portraits two of the kids did of you, Doc," Janice said.

Doc looked around sheepishly while we laughed.

"Hey, any you guys got twenty bucks on you?"

It began the way most miracles do: by accident or the hand of God, take your pick.

It might have been the weather, at least partly. For December, the day had been almost balmy and warm. You know, sweaters instead of heavy coats. No mittens in sight.

Then there were Christmas lights on the stores, and that little bunch of Girl Scouts out raising money in front of the Read Me Now bookstore. Jasper Blankenship was inside going through the books to fortify his cabin's library for winter and sat, listening with a smile to the girls as they laughed and waited for customers that weren't really coming along too briskly.

"It's a shame there aren't more people out today for those girls," said Sarah McKinley, behind the counter. Jasper nodded and paid for his books, then walked out to the truck. He stopped and thought for a while, then brought out his violin, rosined the bow, and walked over to the sidewalk next to the girls.

"You girls like fiddle music?" he asked.

"Sure do."

And Jasper began playing fiddle tunes.

Carla Martinez was driving down the street, headed for the Soup 'R Market when she saw the Girl Scouts dancing with each other in front of their table to Jasper's music. Before he'd had time to finish that tune, she'd returned with her guitar and joined the fun. Jim Albertson, the elementary school principal, showed up with a harmonica, and he wasn't bad at it.

Dud got out his accordion and was able to at least do the bass buttons as accompaniment.

By this time, it was getting dark in the street, and several people turned headlights on the area in front of the bookstore. Older people had joined the Girl Scouts dancing in the streets, and Delbert Chin from the Chinese restaurant across the street sent one of his girls out with a huge pot of tea and paper cups.

The party was on.

It lasted until the cars headlights began to wear down the batteries, but during its brief lifetime, the street dance and mid-winter party cast a blessing on us all.

It must have been the weather.

Stopping in at the Read Me Now bookstore was really a spur-of-the-moment decision for Marvin Pincus. He actually hadn't thought about it until he looked from the sidewalk into the store and saw two things: Sarah McKinley's smiling face behind the counter, and the sign on the shelves that said "Love and other Fiction."

He walked in, making the jingly on the door ring as he did so.

"Good morning Marvin," Sarah said, brightly.

"And a fine morning it is, Sarah," Marvin said back.

"Help you find something today?"

"Actually, I stopped in to see if I couldn't do something for you, Dear," he said, kindly. "I've noticed you're … well, single, I guess…"

"No secret about that, Marvin. But if you have a friend who is really nice, I'm not interested."

"Oh no. I wasn't going to fix you up. It's just that I thought maybe you could use my fly tying love counseling to kind of help your love life."

Sarah smiled at her friend. "What kind of fly do you think I'd need, Marvin?"

"There's a lot to you that's just below the surface, so I'd be guessing we could start with a nice wet fly … but pretty. So maybe a … let's see …"

He looked her over and held up his hands as if to frame her face.

"A Doctor Burke? No. Fergusun. Definitely a Fergusun. It has that quiet elegance that we need to help you."

"You know I'm going to look it up, don't you, Marvin? And if a Fergusun turns out to be plug ugly, I'm coming after you."

"No problem. It's beautiful."

"So why me?"

Marvin looked at his old friend and sighed. "Sarah, it's because … well, I need a woman client, and you are a friend and you're single, and I thought it would help."

She stared at him. He explained.

"Well, so far all I've had are men clients, you see. I guess Randy's a boy, really, but you know. And everyone knows women are really the ones who need fly tying, I thought you could be …"

"… the guinea pig."

Marvin smiled. "I thought of it more as the first pickle out of the jar."

Oh, we could always just go ask Delbert Chin why he did it, but that would take all the fun out of it. You know. So we sat and sipped at the world dilemma think tank meeting of Everything Important down at the Mule Barn truck stop and talked it over.

It was probably inspired by Jasper Blankenship bringing cookies down from the diggin's and passing them out, along with a compliment for each recipient. Others in town did likewise, including Delbert Chin, whose immaculate Gates of Heaven Chinese restaurant is a favorite for special times. Delbert got in the spirit of cookies and passed out fortune cookies on the street to all concerned, wishing each of us a good fortune. He lit up when he did it, you could see. Maybe that's what happened.

It was less than a week later. Delbert brought out a large glass jar full of water and punched small holes in the lid. He set it on a small table just inside the front door to the Gates and put a sign on it: "World Famous Invisible Golden Trout."

Problem was no one could see the fish. When he was asked about it, he said he caught it in Owens Lake, which is dry. He also added he caught it on a dry fly, naturally.

He had a kind of smirk about his mouth when he answered these questions, but it didn't stop every kid and half the adults in town from coming in and looking in that glass jar to see if they could spot the fish.

It was a tourist lady who finally did it, though. She confronted Delbert directly.

"Sir," she proclaimed, "there's no fish in that jar over there. That's a lie!"

"Oh no!" said Delbert and ran to the jar. "Whew!" he said with relief. "For a while I thought he was gone, you know."

"There's no fish in there!" she said.

"Ma'am," Delbert said. "He's more than eight inches long. You see those little-bitty holes? How you think he's gonna get out?"

When it comes to romance, it's hard to beat ol' Dud.

"Dud Campbell," Anita said the other night, "what are you getting me for Christmas?"

"Now Honey, it wouldn't be a surprise if I told you, would it?"

"That means you haven't bought it yet, doesn't it?"

"Well, I won't say I have and I won't say I haven't, but, uh, don't get in that cupboard out in the garage now..."

"I won't, Dud," she said, purring.

Ten minutes later, Dud was flipping his coffee cup upright and sliding into his place in the line of scrimmage at the philosophy counter of the Mule Barn truck stop.

"I'm dead meat, guys," he said.

We inquired as to why this emotional putrefaction should be setting in, and he said, "I don't have anything for Anita for Christmas and I have no idea what to get her."

"Let's look at this scientifically for a moment," said Steve. "What kinda stuff does she like?"

"Uh … well … "

"You don't know, do you?" said Doc.

"Not a clue."

"Does she read? You can pick up a couple of books."

"I don't really know. I kinda figured I'd learn all that personal stuff about her after we were married."

"You *are* married"

"I know. Never got around to it."

"Does she knit?"

"Beats me."

"I got it," said Herb Collins. "You can get her a gift certificate to a store and let her pick out her own gift."

"She said if I ever did anything so insensitive, she'd brain me with a skillet."

So Dud headed home, only to find the garage door open and Anita standing there holding his brand-new Homelite XL chainsaw. He only had time enough to mumble "Our Father…" when Anita set it down gently and flung herself in his arms.

"Oh Honey, how did you know I wanted a Homelite XL with automatic oiler and a 16-inch bar? I couldn't help myself. I looked in the cupboard and found it. It's just what I've always wanted."

"Well, Darlin'," Dud said in his suavest voice, "I do try to be sensitive to your needs."

The whole thing began right after the first good snow this year. Herb Collins was looking out his window at the point on his small farm where Lewis Creek cuts through a rather steep hill. Neighborhood kids were sledding up there and trying to avoid rocks and one gnarly tree that stuck out. He also noticed that if the kids were successful in avoiding death and destruction, they came to an immediate and violent halt at a submerged log next to the creek.

He brought this up at the next unscheduled-but-daily-anyway meeting of the world dilemma think tank down at the philosophy counter at the Mule Barn truck stop. Some executive decisions were made rather suddenly, and construction began the following day.

Jim Kennedy showed up driving a Bobcat, Doc brought a chain saw, and Steve had his four-wheel-drive pickup with a big chain in it.

At the end of three hours, a long, sloping gentle run began up by the road and looped around two turns, and ended in a gentle upslope on the far side of the frozen creek.

Of course, this activity ruined what snow cover there was, so the kids looked disappointed.

But last week it snowed hard, a good six inches, and the kids went running down to try the new sled run.

It wasn't all that exciting for them. So when Doc and Herb and Dud and Steve showed up, one of the kids politely pointed out to Mr. Collins that they couldn't really get going very fast down that hill on the new run.

"I know that," said Herb. "But see all those other steep runs you have? You can go break your neck on any of them. This run is for a special purpose."

"A special purpose, sir?"

Herb nodded. "Steve? If you please."

And Steve brought out the toboggan from his pickup truck, and the old guys took turns being kids once more down their own sledding run.

Some of us went out to Thrill Hill the other day to watch the fun until the state police were able to come up from the upper end and close it.

That's the only name we have for it around here, and those of us who have exchanged oxygen for carbon dioxide for more than 40 years have grown to believe it's called that because of its one or two icy days each year – like this year – when people attempt to drive on it.

Those of us who still collect hormones believe it was named that because of several remote parking spots on it which give a good view of the valley. Not that too many young folks are admiring the view, if you get my drift.

But the ice was out and thick the other day as our annual game of bumper cars began. To watch the regatta on Thrill Hill properly, you must not park anywhere where a vehicle from the hill can slide into your car. You walk over to the vantage point, which is just behind a clump of pretty stout trees. Then you wait until someone is silly enough to try to drive on it.

Doc brought along his doctor bag, just in case it was needed, and Herb brought snacks.

Strangely, an 18-wheeler crept safely down the hill and into town first, and we all raised our coffee cups in a salute to the driver. But then the cars started down, in their slow-motion dance. You could've put music to it as they spun silently and slowly in a frozen ballet of bumper cars and pinball bounces to the bottom. It was all over in half an hour, when the trooper finally barricaded it at the top.

Doc's bag wasn't needed, and Billy down at the repair shop can now put his kids through college.

Ah, the entertainment of small-town life!

For years now, Herb Collins has been helping Santa by donning the red and the beard and the tassels and waving to passing cars on Christmas Eve out at the Old Fort Road crossing. He takes a bag of candy along, in case anyone cares to stop, and he also takes his daughter Cindy along, because she's always his head elf. Cindy's grown now and has helpers of her own, but this has been a daddy/daughter event for a long time and neither sees any reason to quit.

He had done it a few years and was wondering why he was doing it when one special Christmas Eve, as it snowed, he found his reason.

While he and Cindy stood in full-blown elf gear alongside the road, a pickup pulling a moving trailer pulled up and stopped. Cindy brought the candy over to the truck and Herb reached his hands through the window to shake hands with the young boy and girl who were in there with their dad. Both kids were crying and grinning and grabbing his hands.

"Santa," the father said, "we're moving across the country tonight, and the kids were sure you wouldn't be able to find them since they were between homes."

Herb swallowed. "Now kids," he said, "you know Santa will find you no matter where you are tonight."

"Really?" the girl said.

"Why, sure. So you just be good and help your dad, and I'll find you, don't you worry."

"Oh thank you, Santa!" they said.

Their father mouthed a silent "thank you," and everyone waved as the truck went on down the road toward Christmas.

It must have been the raw wind that made Herb wipe the tears away.

"That made the whole thing worth it," Herb says when he tells of that special night. "That's why I keep going back out there."

Steve had already driven the pickup up to his cabin with the groceries and hay, because he knew the snow was coming. And he was coming up, too, in a few days. Coming for Christmas. A special Christmas.

But he had a few more days of work first, and he worked the cattle, fixed some fence, and then checked the shoes on Ol' Snort, his personal horse. The mountain was white now, at least the top half of it, and finally Steve saddled Snort and they rode out of town toward the snow. He thought he could probably get Snort to the cabin in a horse trailer … snow wasn't that deep yet … but that would take some of the fun out of it. Using a horse trailer would be, well, sensible. But this season calls for fun over good sense, love over practicality. And eye twinkles. Yep, twinkles of the eye went well with saddling a little horse spouting geysers of breath, riding up a mountain when he could be driving, and just having fun with his best friend.

It took four hours, four fun hours, to reach the cabin, tie Snort in his shelter and feed him, and get the fire going enough to start shedding the heavier clothes inside. Steve turned on his battery radio and listened while Rudolph was having his nose so bright, put the coffee water on the stove, and lit the kerosene lamps against the kindness of night.

Then he climbed the ladder into his turret and sipped coffee, looking off over the tops of the black spruces and down into the valley where a cluster of man stars marked the location of the Mule Barn and town and all his friends.

And he heard Snort blow his nose happily as he ate his hay, looked around at the home he had built for himself, and wished himself a Merry Christmas.

Sometimes being a rich man has nothing to do with bank accounts.

If you didn't know what time of the year it was, or what the weather was like, you could tell simply by eavesdropping at the philosophy counter of the Mule Barn coffee shop. Let's give it a try.

"Good to see you here, Doc," said Herb Collins. "That warm water on the battery trick work for you?"

"Thanks, Herb. Yep. I tried it this morning. What's that you got there?"

"Travel thingie. You know it's more than 80 degrees in Guatemala … right *now*?"

"Saw a deal on TV," Dud said. "They're water skiing in Florida. You can go fishing down there all year round."

"You going to Guatemala, Herb?" said Doc.

"Maybe. Been thinking about it. I don't know much Spanish, though."

"All you need to know," said Dud, "is '*Hace mucho calor,*' Herb."

"What's that mean?"

"Sure is hot!"

"I was just thinking yesterday," said Doc, "of the unsung beauty of sweat. You know, we take sweat for granted in summer. Heck, we even dislike it and wash it off."

"That's a fact," Dud said.

"But I think it would be kinda fun to sweat right now. You know, just sit in a hot sun and bask like an old lizard and sip iced tea…"

"… and wear dark glasses," said Herb.

" … and watch girls in bikinis," said Dud.

They looked at him.

"Around here?"

"Well, no. I mean, Guatemala or Florida, you know."

"Yeah," said Herb. "Guatemala."

About that time Loretta came up. "You boys want your coffees topped off, or should I just turn the hose on you?"

They shoved their cups forward and grinned.

"Sale on snow shovels down at the hardware store," said Doc.

"Heard that," said Dud.

Doc had his nose stuck in the paper and had it fanned out from Dewey's coffee mug to Steve's plate of hash browns.

"What's so interesting, Doc?" Steve said.

"All these ads," Doc said. "Everyone's having an after-Christmas sale. Groceries, tools, cars, television sets. All of it."

Herb grinned from down the philosophy counter here at the Mule Barn truck stop. "Make you feel kinda left out, does it, Doc?"

Doc put the paper down and sipped his coffee. "I could have a post-Christmas sale, too. Yes, matter of fact, I believe that's exactly what I'll do."

"I can see it now, Doc," Steve said, grinning, "you could take out someone's appendix in exchange for the spare parts."

"Mirth has its place, Steven me lad," said Doc, starting to twinkle. He's a world class twinkler when he gets going good. "But I'm serious. Why shouldn't a physician have a Christmas special too?"

"I've got it!" Dewey said, "Special this week! Half off on amputations!"

Dewey slapped the counter so hard in laughing that most of our coffee spilled. Loretta had to bring the towel and do refills.

"No boys," said Doc, "my special has to do with skateboards."

"I thought you didn't like them, Doc."

"Don't. I hate 'em. That's where my special comes from. How's this: I'll set any bone broken while skateboarding, and all I'll charge is ....I know ...*half* that skateboard!"

Steve pondered this for a minute. "You know, Doc, if you'd extend that offer to bull riders, your freezer'd be full in no time at all."

If there's one thing you can honestly say about Delbert McLain, it's that he's as persistent as a winter cough. As our chamber of commerce here (he's *it*, you see), his fertile brain never ceases its search to turn a sleepy little valley into a cross between Wall Street and Pittsburgh.

That's part of what was going on in his mind this winter's day as he sat in the rented office the local businesses cough up for each month. On a snowy day like this one, of course, you can never tell when the representative of a foreign auto manufacturer might skid on into town and look around for a good pasture in which to install an assembly plant. And what would happen if Delbert wasn't there, wearing his tie, in the chamber office when that occurred?

The next valley over would experience phenomenal growth and we'd still be left without the "big box" stores.

We would be everlastingly condemned to buying our food at the Soup 'R Market, buying our reading material at the Read Me Now bookstore, and sipping our coffee at the Mule Barn truck stop where the waitresses know everything there is to know about us, whether that's okay with us or not.

But it's a snowy day, and no one has dropped by wanting to subdivide the old Johnson place or anything, so Delbert threw his tie over his shoulder to get it out of the way and took his fly-tying vise out of the desk drawer.

He was in a streamer mood, and smiled as he tied the colorful tails on the longer hooks, dreaming of the retrieves his friends would make in Miller pond for the bass there. Delbert doesn't enjoy fishing, just tying the flies. He likes the streamers better than the bass plugs, even if they don't catch as many fish. They just look classier.

So Delbert went on, tying flies for one way of life, and planning how to bring us to another way of life, and smiling. Because he had no idea he was doing that.

Annette George, owner of the Soup 'R Market, picked up the list of her New Year's resolutions:

1. Replace cracked glass on the meat cooler.
2. Walk two miles each morning before work.
3. Lose 15 pounds by summer.
4. Take a class in Spanish.

She thought about the kind of person she'd be at this time next year with all those things done, and it made her smile. Then she looked out the window at the snow and crossed off number two. "Each morning" was just too … too, *inflexible*. It's always best, she thought to make promises you can keep.

Annette tapped her teeth with the pencil.

The Spanish class was in the city, and with gas prices being what they are … well, she could always pick up a Spanish grammar book at the Read Me Now bookstore. Number 4 reluctantly had a line drawn through it.

You know, that glass has been cracked on the meat cooler for six years now, and it has never caused any kind of health threat. So the line up the glass causes a slight distortion as a shopper looks at a pork chop. So what? And have you seen what they get to replace that glass?

The pencil drew again, slowly but deliberately.

This left number three: lose 15 pounds by summer. This is one she will not scratch off. She remembers sitting by the swimming hole on Lewis Creek last summer watching the kids swimming. Next summer, she'll swim with them. She *will* lose those 15 pounds. How? Well, by ... eating better. Sure. Maybe one of those chocolate milkshake supplements each morning. Well, better not say *each* morning, but ... whenever, you know. And walking. How much? Who knows? But walking.

Yes. Walking. Losing 15 pounds. By summer. She smiled and decided to celebrate with a candy bar. Only one, of course.

Life is good.

Marvin Pincus caught the phone on the third ring. It was Margaret down at the Rest of Your Life retirement home.

"Marvin," she said, "do you make house calls?"

"For what?"

"You know, love counseling ... fly tying."

"Uh, sure, why not? You need some help, Margaret?"

"Not me. I'm calling for George Walker. You know, Pop Walker?"

"Isn't he about 105 years old?"

"Eighty-seven, I think. Can you come over?"

Marvin packed his portable fly-tying kit, put on a necktie and drove to the edge of town, near the park, where the home for old-timers stands.

"Hi Pop," Marvin said, walking into his room.

"Oh hi there, uh ... "

"Marvin."

"Right. Marvin. Sit down. What can I do ya fer?"

"I thought you wanted some love advice from me. You know, the fly tying love advice?"

"Fly tying! That's right. I need the love fly, Marvin. Tie me up one, because I need a date with Opal. That's what you do, right? You tie a fly. I pin it on my shirt, and the girls just go nuts over me, right?"

"Well, Pop, I can do that, but most people want love advice from me, and the fly just kinda goes along with it."

174   "Now why would I be asking a youngster like you for love advice?

You just tie me up that lucky love fly and watch me work. What kind of fly do you think I should have?"

Marvin looked solemnly at the antique leprechaun.

"A spinner, I think. You know, for the all-out graceful last-minute love. I think I'll tie you a spent drake."

"You know what we forgot to do?" Anita asked. Dud shook his head. "We forgot to dig out those promises we made to ourselves on New Years's last year."

"Right," Dud said. He was trying to remember what he'd written down as a promise to himself. Right after dinner is a bad time to be disappointed. "I can't remember where we put them," he said, picking up the Valley Weekly Miracle.

"They're in my desk, silly," Anita said, brightly. "I'll go get them."

Dud put the paper down and looked out the window at the snow where the lawn should be. He felt a little dread coming on. Not a big one, just a regular shrug-of-the-shoulders kinda dread. Do we always promise ourselves the moon and deliver a light bulb?

"Here we go," Anita said, tossing Dud's envelope in his lap. "You want me to read mine first?"

"You mean out loud?"

"Of course."

He grimaced and watched as she opened hers. "Okay," she said. "I promised I'd learn to bake sourdough bread this year and I did. And I promised I'd join the Ladies Literary League and I did that. In May I think. And I promised I'd straighten out the filing system down at the office. Took me until August, but I got that, too, Honey. Okay. Your turn."

Dud opened the envelope. He unfolded the paper carefully.

"Do I have to read all of them? You sure? Well, I promised to memorize the Julida Polka on my accordion."

"And you did."

"Yes. Yes I did. And I promised to build that birdhouse by the window."

"Yep. There's number two."

He sat quietly. "Well, Honey, I promised myself I'd finish writing that murder mystery. You know ... 'Murder in the Soggy Bottoms'?"

"The Duchess and the Truck Driver? Sure."

"I'm nowhere near getting that thing done."

"Some people take years to write books. I read the other day it took Max Evans more than 30 years to write 'Bluefeather Fellini.'"

Dud smiled sadly, and nodded. "That's true I guess."

Yes, he thought, but this book of mine isn't 'Bluefeather Fellini.' And I'm not Max Evans. Maybe by next year.

We can always count on Vince coming up with something new. Vince owns the "gas station gun shop" out on the highway, of course. This innovative combination of businesses occurred when the gas station wasn't really paying all the bills, and Vince has a passion for guns, so the unusual combo worked. You can now buy a quart of 10-30 motor oil and a box of .38 special semi-wadcutters at the same time.

Last year, he offered a combination lube and oil and concealed-carry class for a flat hundred bucks. That worked really well, so we were anxious to see what he came up with for this season's special. Well, we found out. Vince got the ladder out and changed the black plastic letters to read, "Reg. unleaded $2.50, shoot while you wait."

Inside, in the empty garage part (Vince really doesn't want to work on cars any more) he has set up an indoor shooting range, and has two pellet guns ready for customers. So while Vince is out checking their oil and tire pressure and radiator water, the car owner can go in and punch holes in a target. The use of the rifles and pellets is free, but he sells the targets for fifty cents apiece.

And the success?

"Well, that would have to be considered … mixed, I guess," Vince said. "I got a bunch of inexpensive pellets in bulk, so that was a good deal, and I sold a lot more oil, because the guys would ask me to put in a quart so they could shoot a while longer. I think some of them actually let some air out of one of their tires so it would take me longer to get them ready.

"But the results of this would have to be mixed, because of old Pop Walker."

We didn't even know he drove any more.

"He doesn't. He's too old. But they brought him by with a couple of old ladies in the Rest of Your Life retirement home van the other day on the way to doctors' appointments, you know? So Pop goes in and shoots while I'm taking care of the van, and he broke one of the windows in that side door I have."

"I'll have to sell a bunch of targets to pay for that window."

"For me," said Dud, "it was the biscuits. Never had so many in my life as I did this year."

"Mashed potatoes," Steve said. "And gravy. Lots of brown gravy. Gravy oozing here and there all over everything. Love gravy."

"Maizie always gets real butter at Christmas," Bert said. "Puts it on everything. Puts it under everything. Puts it in everything."

"I'll bet the biggest thing she puts it in," said Doc, "is you."

"That's the truth," Bert said during the laughter. "I'm up eight pounds."

"Five here," said Steve.

"Almost ten," said Dud.

We all looked at Doc. With his spare frame, he couldn't gain five pounds if you filled his pockets with rocks.

"Why are you looking at me?"

"Did you gain any, Doc?"

"Tried. Oh how I tried. Just couldn't get 'er done."

"I'm going to start walking every day," Bert said.

"Walking? Don't you know walk is a four-letter word," said Steve the cowboy.

"So is *ride*, Steve," Bert said.

Steve grinned. "Yeah, but it's more fun.

"I'm going to drink lots of water," Dud said. "I hear that's a good way to lose weight. Isn't that right, Doc?"

"Well I heard the same thing," Doc said. "But what I know is, if you're out in the field drinking lots of water, you'll lose weight by walking back and forth to the bathroom."

"You guys could always start waiting on tables," said Loretta, coming by to fill our coffee cups. "That would leg you up quite well."

"You look real good, Loretta," Dud said. "I'll bet you never had a weight problem."

"You'd be wrong. You didn't know me when I had that weight problem. I once had to lose 180 pounds to stay healthy."

We were astonished. Bert spoke for all of us.

"You? You have to be kidding! How did you lose 180 pounds?"
She grinned and winked at us. "Got a divorce."

When old Jasper Blankenship came to town from the diggings recently, we asked him over for a few days. He saw us working the home computer and asked about it, but he really seemed to be immune to its wonders.

But then my wife showed him how he could call up a certain program, tell it where he wanted to go, and have it zoom in from outer space to some tiny corner of the world.

Well look out now, boys and girls; we have created a monster!

Ol' Jasper went from being shocked to being a semi-almost-darn-near technogeezer in about half an hour.

For the next three days, we had to wait until the old boy went to sleep before we could check our email. He was on that machine constantly.

But his new ability to eavesdrop on any place on earth at least led to some wonderful stories.

"Come here and look at this," he'd say. We did.

"You see that tree right there? I killed a huge buck under that tree."

"See this? No ... this little cabin over here on the left. That's where old Leroy What's-his-name lived back when I was a kid. He's the one showed me how to pan for gold. Right there in the creek. No ... down a little ways farther, not that close to the cabin. Let me move it a bit ... yeah, right there. See that big hole in the creek? Right there. Got a little bit of color, too. Not much, but if you're a kid and find any gold at all, it's a wonderful thing, you know?"

So for three days we took a tour of Jasper's past. Canyons and creeks and small towns and even the homes where certain special young ladies had lived more than half a century earlier.

It was a fascinating blend of history and technology.

One of the problems Marvin Pincus discovered about running the Fly Tying Love Center here in the valley is that there appeared to be more fly tying than love counseling going on.

This particular morning he was whipping up a nice fluffy Adams dry on a number 12 and wishing everyone's love problems were as easy to solve as tying one of these. He realized he's a pioneer in the field of combining fly tying and romance solutions, but that doesn't mean he couldn't quietly hope for his neighbors to have more love problems. His advice had worked well with Dewey (a lead-wire-wrapped wooly bugger leading to the suggestion he showers *before* he asks a girl out on a date), and with Randy Jones (a pheasant-tail nymph and a Parmachene Belle sending him on his way to girlfriend happiness with Katie Burchell). But there were others out there. There *had* to be others.

Other advice counselors, the ones who just sat there taking notes, managed to find any number of unhappy potential love victims, but the Fly Tying Love Center was noticeably short of them at the moment.

"Marjorie," Marvin said over coffee, "maybe if I offered an incentive, you know? Some little extra that would bring them in for advice?"

"Like what, Honey?"

"Maybe taking some flies that I tied for them and making earrings out of them?"

"The men around here don't really take to wearing earrings."

"I mean, for the women … you know. Women are the emotional ones who need love advice the most. Everyone knows that."

"How many clients have you had so far?"

"Well, three."

"And they were …?"

"Men, true. But I'm not sure what I could offer the guys except the flies themselves to use to go fishing."

"That sounds good."

"And the earrings?"

"We could get you some of those fasteners for the earrings, and it would probably be a good idea to cut the points and barbs off them."

"Good idea."

"And I could wear a pair just to start the neighbor ladies talking about it."

"Yeah! Good idea! I'll tie you up a few right now."

"In that case," Marjorie told her husband, "I've got the ladies club luncheon today and I planned to wear the red outfit…"

"Royal Coachman streamers on number fours! Honey, you're the best."

Anita Campbell watched as her husband, Dud, quietly built a fire in the fireplace. She was still a fairly new bride, but she had learned at least this much of his body language by now, and fixed two cups of coffee. Fire, coffee, evening equals serious talk.

"It was us getting married that did it," he said, finally. "I want you to know I'm really happy being married to you."

"Well thank you, sir," she said, smiling, "but our marriage did what, exactly?"

"Got me thinking about the book."

Oh, the book. *Murder in the Soggy Bottoms,* which Doc said sounded like a young mother with too many diapers. The rest of the local world referred to his book as "The Duchess and the Truck Driver."

"What about the book, Hon?" she asked.

"Maybe I should tone down the murders and put more love in it. I mean, after all, the duchess and the truck driver had a dukelet together, even though the truck driver doesn't know it and he married someone back home and had a daughter, and the daughter wants to marry the dukelet because she doesn't know he's her half brother, and the dukelet likes her, too. So instead of their parents being murdered, what if they get together again?"

Anita sipped her coffee and smiled. "I've always liked love stories better than murder mysteries, myself."

"But you see, I have all these murders ... I'm down to just six of them throughout the book. So if I have a happy ending for the duchess and the truck driver, that cuts me back to just four murders, and then I'll have to figure out if they'll live in her castle just outside Budapest, or at his place back home. Then I'll have to figure out who killed those other people before I get to the end of the book because I can't have it be the same guy as before because that would wreck the romance, you see."

"I know you'll figure it out, Dud," she said, putting her arm around him.

The strain of the creative demon in him showed plainly in his furrowed brow. It used to be so easy to just do his job and come home each night, but literature makes a guy's brain hurt.

"I can't stand winter," said Herb Collins, who had dropped in at the Mule Barn's philosophy counter for a quick cup. "There's nothing to do."

"Get out and enjoy it," suggested Doc. "Go skiing. Go ice fishing. Build a snowman. Do something. Then you'll feel better."

"I don't think your advice will take," said Dud. "Herb seems to be intransigent on this one."

We all looked at Dud.

"You see, he said he couldn't stand winter," Dud continued, "which shows he has a proclivity for intransigence on that particular subject."

We looked at him some more.

"If he were to take up a winter hobby," he continued, "he could stop being intransigent and enjoy things more."

Even Herb was staring at him now.

"I usually," said Herb, "enjoy a proclivity in that direction, but winter is pretty boring, so maybe I really should be intransigent on this point."

"Well Herb," said Dud, "even though you might have a proclivity this season for being intransigent on your attitude about winter, you could kinda ease up and consider a hobby. That way you'd be showing a proclivity for transigence."

"Transigence?" said Doc. "I thought those were people who lived under bridges. You might want to look that one up, Dud."

Dud blushed as we laughed.

"Say Dud?" said Steve, the cowboy. "Wasn't proclivity last month's word?"

"Yes," said Dud, "and I believe I've used it a couple of dozen times already."

"And now this month's word is intransigence, right?"

Dud nodded.

"Well then," said Doc, "it looks like you are going to have a proclivity for saying intransigence this month. That's a veritable plethora of proclivity my friend."

Dud pulled out a pencil and grabbed a napkin.

"How do you spell it, Doc?"

"Spell what?"

"Plethora."

We just groaned. Sometimes education can be ugly.

Bert came waltzing in to the Mule Barn truck stop the other day in high spirits. We knew we were in for yet another lecture. Sure enough.

Even as he pulled up a chair at the philosophy counter and world dilemma think tank, he started in.

"The world, gentlemen," he said. "The world is cresting on a multiplicity of inventiveness at the moment and I'm flat in the middle of it!"

He talks like that sometimes.

We all pretended we hadn't heard him and sipped our coffee.

We're like that sometimes, too.

"Maizie got it for me for Christmas," he said, looking at us as he flipped his coffee cup to the upright and ready-for-filling position.

Finally, Dud couldn't stand it any more. "What was that, Bert?"

"It's the Rat Zapper!" he said. "The cutting edge in domestic varmint control. The computer age has finally come to the wonderful world of pest whacking, people."

"What do you think?" said Doc. "Think he's going to tell us about it anyway?"

A general nod of agreement. "OK, Bert, what the heck is a rat zapper?"

"That's Rat Zapper, capital letters, Doc, 'cause it's a brand name. You see, you just plug this little box into the wall and put it behind something. When the rat goes in and tries to eat the bait, he steps on this metal plate and is electrocuted. You just take it out and dump it and reset it.

"The first thing you do, though, is put some bait in it and let him go get it without the electricity, then you plug that baby in, and ZAP! Oh man, it's just great!"

"High tech rat killin'?" Doc said.

"Oh, you bet. And not only that, but for a little extra, you can have the trap ring your cell phone to let you know when you've caught one. And you can get a whole network of these thingies and they'll each call you when they have a fried rat for you. Isn't that amazing?"

"Well, Bert," I chimed in, "I didn't realize you had a rat problem over at your place."

"I don't," he said, looking discouraged. "But you know, if I put some corn out, maybe by spring....?"

Bob and Carol Burchell pulled into their driveway during the snowstorm, and were surprised to see their daughter, Katie, along with her boyfriend, Randy Jones, sitting on the porch swing, wrapped in a blanket. Both were shivering and smiling.

They followed her parents inside, and in minutes had some hot soup inside them. Randy and Katie watched a couple of television programs together, and then Randy said goodnight and walked home.

"Randy seems to be a really nice boy, Honey," Carol said.

"Thanks, Mom. I like him a lot."

Bob sat quietly, sucking on a cup of evening coffee as though it were dessert. He had a puzzled look on his face.

"Everything OK, Dad?" Katie said.

"Oh ... sure." He took another sip. "It's just ... well, I think maybe one of you doesn't show a lot of good sense."

Katie looked surprised.

Bob explained. "You see, it's one of those what's-wrong-with-this-picture things. Here you have a perfectly warm house, you have a key to the house, and here are two seemingly intelligent young people wrapped in a blanket to keep from freezing to death, sitting out on a frozen steel porch swing. Is that a smart thing to do?"

"No it isn't," Katie said. "That's what I told him. I said we could go in and get something to eat where we'd be comfortable. All he'd let me do is get that blanket."

"That was his idea, freezing on the porch?"

"Yes," Katie said, smiling. "Randy said if we went in the house before you two got home, it might hurt my reputation, and he wasn't willing to risk that."

Katie went into the other room. Bob looked at Carol and smiled.

"You know," he said. "I think I kinda like that boy."

Dud sat perched on the little board at the top of the run, sliding his super-long, super-wide skis slowly back and forth on the snow. He looked down at the people waiting at the bottom. The bottom, a quarter mile away, nearly, but only seconds in Olympic time.

"Representing the United States of America," the announcer said, the sounds reverberating across the mountain peaks, "Dudley Campbell."

The crowd roared and Dud continued psyching himself up. This wasn't just for him, or for his country. This was for Doc and Herb and Marvin, who were too old to do this. For Steve and Dewey, who weren't athletic enough to do this. For his own Anita, who would have things to tell at the Ladies Literary League back home after this.

A moment in time. A moment in a life. Dud smiled and slipped off the board and into his crouch, his arms behind him as the skis rocketed down, faster and faster toward the lip of the jump. And then, at precisely the right time, Dud lifted off, spread his skis into a V and flew. He flew, he soared and didn't seem to land. He flew past the first marker, he flew past the second marker … the one his competitors had been trying to reach all morning, and he landed on clean snow in an area he knew meant a new world record.

A new world record for his country. Tears came to his eyes as he heard the crowd begin to chant "Dud … Dud … Dud…"

"Honey," Anita said, "wake up. Here's some coffee for you." Dud smiled, because he knew this should really be champagne. He did it. You couldn't tell him he didn't.

In the background, the television was softly chattering " … his country's main hope for a medal in men's figure skating…"

Dud smiled and laced up his skates before setting out on the ice. He wasn't nervous. He had trained for this moment for years….

Doc was just getting up to leave the philosophy counter as Herb walked in. Herb was grinning and flexing muscles and had the look of eagles in his eyes. We stared.

"Herb," said Doc. "You know, you can overdo a good thing."

"Why Doc … whatever do you mean?"

"I realize that getting more exercise is your resolution for the new year, but a man your age … you need to pace yourself a little, that's all. Don't try to get in shape all at once."

"Why Doc, I've never felt better in my life. Hey, you were so right to get me on this exercise kick. I've been meaning to thank you. It's just what I've been needing. What would you think about my playing some football in the spring? I mean, it's just touch football, but I miss the ol' razz-matazz, you know?"

Doc shook his head sadly and walked out. Herb started laughing and sat down with us and flipped his cup over for his morning eye opener.

"What was that all about, Herb?" Dud asked.

"A little joke I'm playing on Doc, that's all," Herb said. "You remember how Doc has been on my case to get more exercise and slim down some? Well, there was only one way to shut him up, so I started running. I bought a sweat suit and started running. I run past his house each morning. Then, about an hour later, I run past his house the other direction, huffing and puffing and looking at my watch."

"An hour? You run for an hour each morning?"

"Of course not," Herb said, laughing. "I run past Doc's house then walk the block to the library. An hour later, I run past Doc's house and then walk two blocks home."

We stared at him.

"What?" he said. "You know Doc's going to worry about me one way or the other. I just thought I'd change it up a bit."

Marvin Pincus usually has something to say about almost everything, and this time it was skiing. He was stopped, there on Parker's Ridge, our local ski slope, resting his arms on the antique wooden ski poles he'd used since the Coolidge Administration.

Down the hill came youngsters, swooping and swooshing on snowboards, cutting roostertails of powdery snow, and setting ol' Marvin to shaking his head.

"When I was young, we had to work at this, you know," he said, his breath rising like geysers of human antiquity. "First of all, you had to take skiing lessons. It wasn't easy, because of course you had to wait until there was snow. Then you had to learn fast so you could be a skier before it all melted. Then you had to buy the right equipment and practice learning to stop and turn. When you got really good at it, you could go out and pick up a handful of snow, squeeze it in your hand, and tell exactly what kind of wax to use on your skis."

He shook his head. "But now we have these snowboards. It sure does look like a lot of fun, I must admit, but near as I can tell, all you need to get started in that sport is an idiot and a six-pack."

The banner across the front of the Read Me Now bookstore said

"Happy Anniversary, Jimmy and Liz! Giant Sale on Love Books!"

We walked by the bookstore for a couple of days before Doc finally went in to talk with Sarah McKinley, who owns the place. After several days of speculation down at the Mule Barn truck stop, none of us could recall any local couple known as Jimmy and Liz. We hated to admit defeat, but there was just no getting around it. We thought Doc would be the perfect one to find out about the mysterious couple.

When Doc walked up to the counter, Sarah was ready for him with one of those Mona Lisa smiles. Oh … she knew. She knew all right.

"Hi there Sarah," said Doc. "Big sale, huh?"

"It's the season, Doc. Love books. Right over there in the 'Love and other Fiction' department. You need some love books?"

"Well, not really, Sarah. It's just that we've been trying to figure out who Jimmy and Liz are and we haven't been successful, so the boys thought…"

"Now Doc, don't tell me you didn't realize that Feb. 16 was the Monroe's wedding anniversary."

"Monroe?"

"Sure. You remember. James Monroe? Monroe Doctrine? Keep foreign influence out of the Western Hemisphere? Jimmy married Elizabeth Kortright on February 16 in 1786."

"President Monroe?" Doc shook his head. "I hate to spring this on you, Sarah, but I'm too young to remember when Jimmy and Liz got married."

"She was only 18 you know."

'Well, no, I didn't realize that."

"They were married in New York. It was a big deal at the time."

"Are you … related to them, maybe?"

"No. Just thought it would be nice to celebrate their anniversary with a sale on love books."

Doc smiled. "Well, now, we'll all raise our cups to Jimmy and Liz down at the Mule Barn tomorrow morning."

Sarah smiled. We're still trying to figure her out, you know.

"Two hundred and twenty-two years," Sarah said, as Doc left the store. "And they said it wouldn't last…"

Bob Milford popped in for a cup the other day at the philosophy counter of the Mule Barn truck stop. Bob isn't usually seen in town during the day, as he's manager of the big Diamond W spread, and there are lots of daylight things to do out that way.

As we worked our way through the usual topics: women, politics, laundry and welding, Bob said he's planning a spring turkey hunt.

We nodded, silently vowing to check our own camo clothes and slate turkey calls.

"I sure hope this season goes better than last one, though," Bob said, sipping his coffee.

"Didn't you get a turkey, Bob?" asked Doc.

"Well, yes and no, I guess you could say, Doc. It's just the way it happened that didn't turn out so well. You see, I was driving the stock truck out the highway …."

"What happened, Bob?" asked Dud, finally.

"Oh, this stupid turkey flew out of the woods and across the highway. That wasn't bad in itself, but there was this state trooper behind me, you know? I kept watching him to see if he thought I was doing something wrong. You know how it is. I checked my speed, made sure my seat belt was on real good. I kept looking in the rearview mirror at him, but even if I hadn't, I couldn't have stopped it …."

He took another sip and looked up at us.

"You know the headache rack on the stock truck? Well, that dumb turkey pulled up when he saw the truck, but he didn't clear that rack and smacked it hard. He went up and over and came right down through the windshield of that cop car. Smashed it all to pieces."

"Bummer," said Dud, who tried to be a hippie once.

"The worst part was, the trooper gave *me* a ticket for it!" Bob said.

"A ticket? For what?"

Bob smiled. "Flippin' him the bird."

Daybreak. Coffee. The Big Two.

There's something so satisfying about getting out of bed when the world is still dark and quiet and resting. Making the coffee gives us time to scratch and think. Well, scratch, anyway. Most of that thinking will start after about the third cup of coffee.

But it's a quiet time. A private time. When the world is dark, and there isn't yet a hint of pink over the eastern mountains, it's very good.

We can relax. No one is expecting anything from us right now. Our guilt can take some time off, and we can listen to music or work a crossword puzzle or turn on the TV and watch the weather guy discuss millibars and troughs.

Soon enough, we'll have to be out there living for others: our bosses, our customers, our animals, our fields. But right now no one needs us except the dog, and she does well on kibbles and an ear rumple.

We can look out the window at the eastern glow and wonder what will happen in the hours until our world turns dark again. People will be born and people will die. People will win honors and people will go to jail. People will create things today that live past them and people will disappear forever. People will write about these things and other people will read about these things.

And then the world will go dark on us again and we'll think about what happened in our tiny portion of this huge moving amalgam and hopefully we'll sleep easily tonight. Then, when we arise tomorrow and head for the coffee pot, we can think about what happened today, and how it has made us slightly different for taking on the next tomorrow.

Come to us, daylight. Bring us the new day. But do it gently, please, and slowly enough for one more cup.

Did you have fun?

I put this part at the back of the book on purpose. Didn't want to clutter up the beginning with it. Hopefully by this time you've read the columns we stuck up there in front for you. This part isn't a column, so if you guessed wrong about that, and it made you throw something at the cat, you're free to quit now. Or you can stick around a few minutes for some personal fiddle-faddle.

This is the part where a writer usually tells you how wonderful he is. But since only my bluetick hound, Sadie, believes that, we'll jump right into something else.

Like where *Home Country* came from.

I've been attempting to commit journalism since 1964, when, at the tender age of 22, I was given the difficult mission of interviewing showgirls at Lake Tahoe for the *Tahoe Daily Tribune*. Strangely enough, after that baptism of fire, I stuck with newspapers for the next 152 years or so. In that time, I've been editor of a few small papers and even owned a couple of *very* small papers in Alaska for a while. The point being that, during all that time, I thought a column celebrating American life would be a fun thing to have. Other columnists shout things like "Vote the way I do or roast in hell, sucker!" or "Apologize to your mother-in-law or roast in hell, sucker!" or "Believe me when I tell you the Mets will win the series or roast in hell, sucker!"

Well, I was never sure enough of my roast-in-hell beliefs to want to foist them off on anyone else. Besides, there's just the off chance I could be wrong, and that would be embarrassing.

So I was talking with my dad one day in 2003 or maybe it was 2004 (we spoke to each other during both those years, so it's kinda hard to pin it down), and I was expressing to him what a nice thing it would be for small papers to have a column that was fun, non-controversial, and free.

At this point, you might as well know that he and I shared genes and chromosomes, but not political beliefs. One of us was slightly to the left of Chairman Mao and the other slightly to the right of Genghis Khan.

Pop said a column such as I described was impossible for the simple fact that no one … *no one* … could write a non-controversial column. Oh, he said, one might try for a column or two, but before very long, the roast-in-hellers would emerge, because it goes against human nature for a guy with a typewriter to keep his stupid politics to himself.

Well, that did it. There were flags all over the field, campers. The gauntlet had been slapped across my journalistic face and I decided to prove him wrong.

So then I had to figure out what the needs of a small-town newspaper editor (which I used to was) might be. In the newsroom, the two words that are spoken most often (except for "coffee's ready") are "space problems." This has nothing to do with astronauts, but is the common headache when an editor has to decide whether the ladies club luncheon or the Girl Scout parade hits the old wastebasket because there just isn't room for both.

So the column, I said wisely to myself, would have to be short. I decided 350 words, give or take, would allow me to spell most of the words right and still express a thought.

I've been a columnist for most of my career, so keeping things short wasn't too much of a problem. I've written columns for the largest papers in Alaska and New Mexico, and for two national magazines, *Petersen's Hunting* and *New Mexico Magazine*, so I didn't jump into this without at least knowing how challenging it could be.

Home Country, also, is fiction. But it is fiction based on people you know and so do I. Being fiction gives a guy a lot more room to have fun.

Yes, I write novels, too. In fact, that's where I learned how much fun it is to be fictional. Hey, if you don't like a character in your book, kill him!

Ah ... the *power!*

A little aside here. Remember the column where Delbert Chin drags people back into the kitchen of his restaurant to see how clean he keeps it? When that column ran, I heard from editors in Alaska, Tennessee, Florida, New Mexico and Illinois, saying they received calls wanting to know just where in town the Gates of Heaven Chinese joint was. That was fun.

(If you own a Chinese joint called Gates of Heaven, I'll expect free egg rolls for the plug.)

In the *Home Country* columns, the characters are fictional, but the Mule Barn truck stop actually exists. I'm a regular there for coffee and problem solving. It's called Murphy's Mule Barn and it's on Second Street at the extreme northern end of Albuquerque, in case you want to go there someday. I didn't think it would hurt any to use the name of a real truck stop. They can give you a saddle-blanket-sized chicken-fried steak with enough cream gravy to stop your heart before you can pay for it. And no, I have to pay for my coffee, same as everyone else. No special deals.

But the biggest problem came when I tried to figure out how to get paid for writing the column. Always, throughout journalistic history, syndicated columnists have been paid so much a month by each paper for the rights to print the column. So if you get three bucks apiece each week from a thousand papers, hey, the beer's on you, Jack.

But that's not what I wanted to do because 1. that's how everyone else does it, and I'm just a little bit stubborn, and 2. I have yet to meet a small-town newspaper editor who wanted to pay three bucks for anything. So I came up with the idea of having a sponsored column. Provide it free to the paper, with the stipulation that they print a little bold-faced tag line at the end, saying something like **Brought to you by Joe's Hardware**. Get paid by Joe, see? The problem was finding Joe, of course.

Some editors weren't happy with this plan at first. It was the old question of "We've never done it that way before." One guy was really hot. He wrote me back saying that if he were going to put a tag line in his paper like that, ol' Joe would have to pony up hard cash for the space because the whole thing stank and went against all his Puritanical paid-advertising ethics.

Fortunately, others didn't feel that way.

I reminded the editors how we used to use prepared fillers back when

191

I was on the desk. These were really fun, and were especially needed back in the days of hot lead. We had more holes to fill in those days. Some outfits sent out free sheets of fillers to papers everywhere. One of the biggest filler producers was the American Pie Filling Institute. I'm not making this up. Ask any editor with gray hair.

So when a story came up short by an inch or so, and we needed something to fill that hole so the ads wouldn't slam into each other, we'd look through the filler pages and pick one out that fit about right and plug it in. That's why you'd sometimes see, right after the story about the church bazaar, something like this: "George Washington was the first President of the United States, according to the American Pie Filling Institute." Well, I have it on good authority that George was our first President whether or not the American Pie Filling Institute gave its blessing, but there you go. I figured if editors didn't mind plugging pie filling, (and pie filling is still being used, by the way) they probably wouldn't complain about Joe's Hardware.

And they didn't.

So today, it is more than six years since I set out to prove Pop wrong, and it has been fun. Even Pop was amazed that I could write a non-controversial column. The readers enjoy our characters and have come to know and laugh at Doc and Steve and Marvin and Annette and all the others. So have I.

At this writing (January, 2012), the column is printed weekly in 236 papers nationwide with a readership of just under two million. And it grows a bit each month. That beats the tar out of any projections I might have made when we started. We lost Pop just over a year ago, but I know he was happy to have been proven wrong this time. It didn't happen that often.

Are the columns more along the lines of "our lives the way they ought to be"? Sure. Most of the time, anyway. Why? Because I like it that way.

And it's my typewriter.

(Well, you know it's a computer, right? And the column wouldn't be possible unless it could be disseminated by email, too.)

So, will I be able to write the column more gooder in the future? Of course. I'm only 69 ½ years old, so give me some time to practice, okay? We'll do our best.

Thanks for visiting *Home Country*. You're always welcome here. Come back often.

Slim Randles — www.slimrandles.com

About the author:

Slim Randles learned mule packing from Gene Burkhart and Slim Nivens. He learned mustanging and wild burro catching from Hap Pierce. He learned horse shoeing from Rocky Earick. He learned horse training from Dick Johnson and Joe Cabral. He learned humility from the mules of the eastern High Sierra.

For the last 40 years or so, he's written a lot of stuff, too, especially in his *Home Country* column, which is syndicated all across this country.

He lives in Albuquerque, New Mexico, and in a small cabin in the middle of nowhere at the foot of the Manzano Mountains.

CPSIA information can be obtained at www.ICGtesting.com
Printed in the USA
LVOW122214011112

305525LV00001B/3/P